KT-367-436

Contents

vocational nurses. Professional registered nurse programs: the baccalaureate degree. Graduate education. Nontraditional approaches. Selecting a school. Financial assistance.

The importance of self-assessment. Potential employment sources. Preparing a résumé. The interview.

Nursing service. Nursing administration. Nursing education. Nursing research. Military and volunteer nursing. Nursing practice specialties.

American Nurses Association. National League for Nursing. International Council of Nurses. Sigma Theta Tau. Academy of Nursing.

OPPORTUNITIES

in

Nursing Careers

REVISED EDITION

KEVILLE FREDERICKSON

VGM Career Books

Chicago   New York   San Francisco   Lisbon   London   Madrid   Mexico City
Milan   New Delhi   San Juan   Seoul   Singapore   Sydney   Toronto

The *McGraw·Hill* Companies

Library of Congress Cataloging-in-Publication Data

Frederickson, Keville.
    Opportunities in nursing careers / Keville Frederickson.—Rev. ed.
        p.   cm.—(VGM opportunities series)
        Includes bibliographical references.
    ISBN 0-07-140585-2
        1. Nursing—Vocational guidance—United States.   I. Title.   II. Series.

    RT82 .F66   2003
    610.73'06'9—dc21   2002033148

1 2 3 4 5 6 7 8 9 0   LBM/LBM   2 1 0 9 8 7 6 5 4 3

ISBN 0-07-140585-2

Interior design by Rattray Design

McGraw-Hill books are available at special quantity discounts to use as premiums and sales promotions, or for use in corporate training programs. For more information, please write to the Director of Special Sales, Professional Publishing, McGraw-Hill, Two Penn Plaza, New York, NY 10121-2298. Or contact your local bookstore.

This book is printed on acid-free paper.

Foreword

"Extra! Extra! Read all about it . . . 'Nursing—The Hottest Profession You'll Ever Love,'" shouted the young boy, a large sack of newspapers flung halfway across his back. "I'll take one," said Michael, a high school junior. "Thank you," said the young boy as coins were exchanged for the newspaper. Michael, who was going to school, made his way to a seat in the crowded subway car and pulled the newspaper from his knapsack. "What's so great about nursing?" he mused as he unfolded the paper. Michael was considering premed, but he was concerned about the time and cost of going for a medical degree. His high school guidance counselor had told him that he could meet his goals in less time and with less expense by attending nursing school. Michael wanted to know more.

He read "Nursing—The Hottest Profession You'll Ever Love" and learned that there was a shortage of registered nurses and that the job market for nursing was wide open. "By the year 2020 there

Note: "Nursing—The Hottest Profession You'll Ever Love" is the theme of the 2003 National Student Nurses Association Annual Convention.

will be a projected 40 percent increase in demand for registered nurses to care for a growing population, as well as a larger proportion of elderly persons," stated the article. "I'll always have a job," pondered Michael, as he reviewed the list of nursing specialties and references for further information.

Eager to learn more, Michael purchased the book you are about to read. He also visited websites such as discovernursing.com, where he found a searchable database for nursing schools and nursing scholarships; and the National Student Nurses Association Career Center on nsna.org. From the *Occupational Outlook Handbook*, U.S. Department of Labor, Bureau of Labor Statistics (http:// stats.bls.gov/oco/ocos083.htm), he learned that nursing is:

- the largest health care occupation, with more than two million jobs
- one of the ten occupations projected to have the largest number of new jobs
- a profession with very good job opportunities
- a profession that offers earnings that are above average, particularly for advanced practice nurses, who have additional education or training

Convinced that nursing *is* a hot career choice, he began to think of the next big decision—where to go to nursing school. Selecting the right nursing program is as important as actually deciding to become a nurse. There are so many programs to choose from, he thought, as he examined the possibilities. He did not stop with the selection of an undergraduate program; he began to think about graduate education and going for a doctorate in nursing, so that he could become a nurse researcher or teach in a college or university.

Wanting to know more, Michael contacted a local nursing school and asked about the prerequisites to get into the nursing program. The requirements were very similar to those for premed—a strong background in the sciences, chemistry, physics, anatomy, and physiology. He would need a grade point average of at least 3.0 to enter the more competitive programs. The nursing courses sounded really interesting, with a lot of time spent in clinical settings actually delivering patient care. This was very appealing to Michael, who dreamed of making a difference in people's lives. He learned this about himself when his father was diagnosed with cancer. A nurse had made all the difference in the final days of his father's life, and this had left a strong impression on Michael.

Nursing makes a difference in the lives of many people. Once you have made your decision to be a registered nurse, you'll soon realize the best news of all—that nursing *is* the hottest profession you'll ever love. Go for it!

Diane J. Mancino, Ed.D., R.N., CAE
Executive Director
National Student Nurses Association

Acknowledgments

I WOULD LIKE to express my sincere appreciation to Christine Reitman for her enthusiasm and assistance in the preparation of this book and to my husband, Robert Tomasson, and my son, Hale, for their patience and support.

I would also like to thank both the American Nurses Association and the National League for Nursing for their cooperation in furnishing some of the essential materials and data cited in this book.

1

A BROAD VIEW OF NURSING

THE ART AND science of nursing, as it is today, began with the work of Florence Nightingale in the 1850s. Before this the care of the ill and infirm was provided by various groups. Both the nature of the treatment and the treatment provided were determined by the historical climate.

The Roots of the Profession

In ancient times there was some knowledge of nursing, and treatment included instruction in such areas as personal hygiene, illness communicability, and the art of medicine. For example, Babylonian medical tablets unearthed in 1849 indicated that illness was treated with measures like diet, rest, bandaging, and enemas.

It is interesting that proper hygiene was advocated by many ancient cultures. The Egyptians in particular formulated regulations about bathing and proper diet. The Chinese made a number of early contributions, although many of their opinions about illness, like those of other civilizations, were based on their belief in the presence of demons and spirits. The early Chinese used charms for the prevention of illness. At the same time they demonstrated some degree of sophistication—female obstetricians assisted with the births of babies, and a book was written about the circulatory system. Probably the most well-known Greek in the field of medicine is Hippocrates. He is best remembered for the Hippocratic Oath, which states that the physician should hold himself responsible for high ethical standards.

Before Christianity, the ill often were cared for by temple attendants, priest-physicians, and medicine men. With the advent of early Christianity, groups of individuals were organized to provide certain charitable nursing services to the sick and infirm. These groups were made up primarily of widows, virgins, and deaconesses, who eventually donned religious clothing or habits to identify them and their work. Their goals were very idealistic and were based on serving God. Records indicate that most of these individuals would perform any task, and the more menial and humiliating the chore, the greater the reward. Lowly tasks seemed to function as penance to erase sins. Concurrently with such groups, the need for hospitals as formal settings arose, and they began to be established throughout Europe.

The Renaissance in the fourteenth century brought an increase in the spirit of humanism, with advancements in the fields of the arts and sciences and many new discoveries. However, these findings were not yet applied to the treatment of the sick. The alchemist or druggist and the bloodletting barber-surgeon provided much of the treatment for disease. Interestingly, nursing responsibilities did not vary much from the previous era. They continued to be based on religion and were supported by the church.

During the Reformation of the sixteenth century, service to the sick and poor took a decided turn for the worse. With the de-emphasizing of religion and lack of charitable dedication, intelligent noblewomen no longer felt compelled to provide nursing services. Since wages were menial, women of low educational and social levels provided hospital and social services. It was in this same atmosphere in the nineteenth century that Florence Nightingale made her decisive and significant contributions, initiating nursing as an entity.

Florence Nightingale was born in 1820 into a well-educated, cultured English family. Her background included influential acquaintances, extensive traveling abroad, and diverse and comprehensive educational experiences. Her interests in public health and the care of the sick developed her reputation in the area of hospital reform; through her work during the Crimean War (1853–56), she established the need for knowledgeable and well-prepared nurses. Following the war, she assisted in establishing a school of nursing that taught principles of public health and methods of caring for the sick. Florence Nightingale's work and the publication of her book in 1859, *Notes on Nursing: What It Is and What It Is Not*, helped establish career education for nurses. Although Florence Nightingale died in 1910, she continued to influence the development of nursing through her writings and schools of nursing.

By the time of the Spanish-American War in 1898, schools of nursing in such places as Boston; New York City; and New Haven, Connecticut; were training nurses who utilized skills and knowledge based on Nightingale's ideas. Since then schools of nursing have greatly multiplied, and currently the large proportion of nursing education takes place within an academic framework. Also, nursing practice has attempted to keep pace with a rapidly changing technology by developing a sound theoretical base that will support nursing changes for the future.

Defining the Art of Nursing

In the United States today there are more than 2.5 million individuals who, when addressed as nurse, will respond. Possibly in no other career is there so much confusion as to educational preparation, job qualifications, job titles, and job descriptions. For example, a hospital hires individuals whose licenses read: "registered professional nurse," "licensed practical nurse," or "licensed vocational nurse." These individuals may have educational credentials from a school of practical nursing, a hospital school of nursing, a community college, or a university. Their educational credentials vary from a diploma or certificate of program completion to a bachelor's degree or even a Ph.D. Once in a hospital setting, the nurse may be called a nurse manager, a nurse researcher, a nurse-midwife, a primary care nurse, or a practical nurse. How confusing this becomes.

It is not surprising that high school students, guidance counselors, beginning students of nursing, and the lay public in general approach the field of nursing with confusion, frustration, and bewilderment.

In part, such confusion is the result of the escalating health care needs of the individual and the needs of society in general. Changes within the nursing profession also contribute to this situation due to increasing technology in both the community and hospital settings. Attempts are being made to bridge the gap between apprenticeship preparation and preparation within institutions of higher education.

Considering the confusion about the career of nursing, definitions vary greatly, depending on who is doing the defining and for what purpose. Probably the most well-known nurse—even today—is Florence Nightingale. In her book *Notes on Nursing: What It Is and What It Is Not*, she attempted for the first time to delineate and describe the elements of nursing. She states that the term *nursing* is quite poorly defined:

> It has been limited to signify little more than the administration of medicines and the application of poultices. It ought to signify the proper use of fresh air, light, warmth, cleanliness, quiet, and the proper selection and administration of diet—all at the least expense of vital power to the patient.
>
> The art of nursing, as now practiced, seems to be expressly constituted to unmake what God had made disease to be, viz., a reparative process.

Much later, in the mid-twentieth century, another nursing leader, Virginia Henderson, stated in her book *The Nature of Nursing*, that nursing is:

> The helping of the patient to do those things leading toward health or a piece of that which he ordinarily would do for himself if he had the necessary strength, will or knowledge, and to help him in such a way that he is able to do for himself as soon as possible.

In the April 1958 issue of *Nursing Outlook*, Dorothy Johnson stated:

> Nursing is a professional discipline and, as such, a social service. It provides a direct service to individuals, a service that offers comfort, gratification and assistance at those times when individuals are under stress and in relation to their basic human needs. In so doing, it fur-

ther offers an indirect service that makes a specific contribution to the promotion and maintenance of health and the recovery from illness. It involves the ability to assess situations, arrive at decisions and implement a course of action designed to resolve nursing problems. It has a two-pronged basis in knowledge—one, knowledge of the predictable patterns of behavior of people under stress within a broad category of variables and two, knowledge of the nursing behavior indicated or, to use the jargon, helpful intervention.

Or, as more simply stated by Thelma Ingles in the September 1959 issue of the *American Journal of Nursing*:

Nursing is the art of helping people feel better—as simple and as complex as this.

Martha Rogers, in her book *An Introduction to the Theoretical Basis of Nursing*, discusses nursing in the following manner:

Nursing practice focuses on human beings—on man in his entirety and wholeness. Nursing diagnosis encompasses the man-environment relationship and seeks to identify sequential, cross-sectional patterning in the life process. Nursing intervention is directed toward repatterning of man and environment for more effective fulfillment of life's capabilities. Life's capabilities encompass man's humanness, his creative promise, his capacity to feel and reason, the symphonic potential of his tangible structure and functioning.

And finally, Rosella Schlotfeldt states in the December 1973 issue of *Nursing Outlook* that in differentiating between the role of the physician and the nurse:

The nurse's primary intellectual concern, and functions related thereto, is that of helping each person attain his highest possible level of general health. . . . The nurse's practice focus is on assessing people's health status, assets, and deviations from health, and on helping sick people to regain health and the well or near-well to maintain or attain health through the selective application of nursing science and the use of available nursing strategies.

In summary, nursing leaders over the past hundred years have stated that the art of nursing should provide an environment conducive to assisting a patient's healing processes while the patient is in a debilitated state. More recently, nursing leaders have advocated active promotion of the highest possible level of health in all individuals. For example, utilizing the theory of self-care enables individuals to take an active part in their health care needs, thereby achieving optimal health.

Legal Definition

One method for defining a particular occupation is to examine its legal definition. This is especially effective when dealing with health-related professions, as state laws are designed to protect the safety of the public by ensuring the maintenance of specified standards.

In nursing, such laws are known as nurse practice acts. Currently there is a movement afoot to alter and revise the existing legal definition in each state to include the spectrum of actions currently considered "nursing." Revision of the nurse practice acts is necessary because the roles and responsibilities nurses are assuming have broadened and have become more complex, particularly as the utilization, numbers, and types of nurse practitioners increase. The nurse practice acts in many states now include provision for diagnosis, drug prescription, treatment, professional accountability, and the conceptual definition of nursing. It has been necessary, therefore, to alter the legal definition to protect both the nurse and the patient. Each state has designed its practice act as a way of guiding the evolving practice of nursing.

Registered nurses utilize substantial specialized knowledge derived from the biological, physical, and behavioral sciences. This knowledge is applied to the care, treatment, counsel, and health instruction of persons who are experiencing changes in the normal health processes or persons who require assistance in the maintenance of health; in the management of illness, injury, or infirmity; or in the achievement of a dignified death. They also perform such additional acts as are recognized by the nursing profession as proper for a registered nurse.

This law truly defines nursing as a more complex occupation than it has been considered in the past. In many ways the field of nursing is in its most exciting era, offering the greatest number of alternatives and diversity in job opportunities. For example, nurses can be found working in physicians' offices, industry, corporations, the community, and various other health-related facilities.

A Broadening Role

Through the definitions proposed by both nursing leaders and the state nurse practice acts, traditional nursing has been significantly altered. Until recently the nurse's role and responsibilities were quite limited. A number of societal influences have resulted in the expanded and more independent role nurses now assume.

Changing Technology

These roles are in part a result of the rapid advancements in technology and scientific discoveries, such as the advent of computerized patient record systems that handle such things as laboratory data and x-ray results. Equipment used for diagnosing and treating disease is now much more sophisticated, complex, and sometimes more frightening to the patient than in the past. For example, eye problems once considered untreatable are now alleviated through the use of a laser beam; previously incurable cancer is now treated in a high-pressure hyperbaric oxygen chamber; brain tumors are now diagnosed and located in their earliest stages using a CAT scan, with surgery done while the patient is awake; and major surgery is performed on an outpatient basis using arthroscopic or laparoscopic instruments that resemble a straw.

As a result of such advancements and changes in the way we pay for health care, patients today undergo more extensive treatment periods, and their needs—physical and emotional—are often greater. Likewise, patients who enter the hospital are much sicker than ever and when nursed at home, require more complicated treatment, such as receiving intravenous medications. Therefore, more nurses than ever before are needed to provide knowledgeable judgment to determine the nature of patient care.

The health care consumer of the 1920s spent little time learning how to remain healthy and prevent disease. In contrast, the current national focus is more on the promotion of health and the prevention of disease. As a result, patients, as educated consumers of health care, are demanding more than treatment for disease, and each time they enter the health care scene, total care is much broader and more complex. In health care reform proposals, nurses will be providing much more of the primary care, especially when it emphasizes prevention of illness, health promotion and diagnosis, and treatment of common health problems. In this role the nurse will need to collaborate with other health care professionals as well as clients and patients.

Changing Population

Another societal factor that has demanded a broader role from the nurse is that of demographic changes in the population. The estimated population in the United States in 1994 was approximately 260 million, up from the 1985 population of 236 million. The U.S. Census Bureau predicts that by the year 2025, more than 20 percent of the population will be over the age of sixty-five. This population consists of the baby boomer generation that will become senior citizens. By the year 2050, 5 percent of all Americans will be older than age eighty-five. Although this represents a marked slowing in the overall increase of the population, of greater significance is the continuing increase in the life expectancy figure and the increase in the number of persons over the age of sixty-five. In 1900 there were little more than three million persons over sixty-five; by 1980 there were more than twenty million elderly. This essentially means that one out of every ten Americans is over sixty-five. The eighty-five and older group is considered the one most rapidly rising—by the year 2000 there were more than 100,000 Americans over the age of one hundred. It has been projected that within a generation, more than 50 percent of the population will be over age fifty.

With the number of elderly increasing so rapidly, nursing has been charged with providing quality care to more elderly and with helping them to arrive at that stage of life in the best possible mental and physical health. Nurses have been prepared to meet such a challenge.

Changing Lifestyle

The current fast-paced, highly stressful style of American life is another area that points to a need for more comprehensive nursing. In his book *Future Shock*, Alvin Toffler has written about the hectic pace that Americans maintain. He talks about the changes that affect an individual's style of life and the mind-boggling pace of technological and scientific advancements.

Experts and researchers are discovering that such change and stress result in tremendous physical and emotional wear and tear on individuals and their relationships. The stress on relationships is one factor experts have linked with the high divorce rate of recent years. In 1990 there was a 1 percent decrease in the number of marriages and a 7 percent increase in the number of divorces in the United States. It has been estimated that currently one out of every three marriages will end in divorce, whereas the ratio was one out of every four just a decade ago.

Nurses are now hired to work with business and industry to monitor employee stress and to detect evidence of early physical or emotional breakdown. They are also responsible for teaching workers about the effects of overwork, anxiety, and tension.

In addition, literature on nursing pressures shows that nurses, too, experience high levels of occupational distress. Researchers attribute this to work stress as well as to environmental factors such as fewer nurses for sicker patients, problem patients, and inadequate equipment, to internal tensions experienced by nurses.

The Expanding Role of Nurses

With the increase in the number of nurses earning master's and doctorate degrees, the area of nursing research is growing rapidly. Some hospitals have created a separate department staffed by nurse researchers. Their function is to design and carry out studies that will improve patient care and encourage optimal health status. For example, one large metropolitan hospital has nurses working together with doctors doing the same treatments for patients suffering from heart failure. One nurse researcher discovered that an ice ring around a patient's head during drug therapy for cancer sometimes prevents the patient's hair from falling out.

The opportunities for an individual choosing a career in nursing are more diverse and exciting than ever before. The role of the nurse continues to evolve to meet the needs of our modern society. A dynamic, independent individual is needed to respond to escalating scientific discoveries and technological advancements in the health care arena. Both extensive and intensive health promotion and disease prevention are needed to counteract the effects of rapid changes and excessive stress on the individual alone and in groups in our society. Well-educated nurses are needed to function in this capacity.

How does nursing translate modern nursing knowledge and skills into practice to meet the health care needs of society? Looking toward the future, the skills nurses will need will definitely change with the needs of the patient population. Nurses must posses the skills to manage care for an increasingly diverse population. Nursing roles will need to expand to accommodate and incorporate advances in technology.

The following are a few portraits that illustrate how and where nursing is provided:

• Jennifer, an R.N., graduated from a four-year baccalaureate nursing program. After one year as a staff nurse at a busy university hospital, she joined the Peace Corps and was assigned to a small hospital in the South Pacific. She was one of two nurses and two physicians, plus an assortment of local workers, assigned to care for 250 patients in the hospital and to provide health care to the people in the neighboring area. Many of her patients were afflicted with malnutrition, leprosy, cholera, or parasitic infections. Jennifer worked a minimum of twelve hours a day and often made home visits to the families in the outlying village settlements. She would evaluate the condition of the entire family and often provide them with food, medicine, vitamins, and soap. Although narrowly missing a poisonous dart from an unfriendly tribe of natives and finding her job at times frustrating, tiring, and discouraging, she reported that it was the most rewarding and exciting experience she ever had.

• Carl, also an R.N., earned his master's degree in psychiatric/mental health nursing after completing an associate degree and then a baccalaureate in nursing. Throughout his nursing career he always enjoyed working with the elderly. He organized and led support groups at senior citizen centers and taught geriatric nursing courses at a school of nursing. Following a campaign on advocacy for the rights of the elderly, he was asked to administer the state health care division in the Office of Aging. He believes that his education has paid off since he uses knowledge about organizations, politics, and the health care system in his job. His latest project was developing a grant for communities to provide home health care at a reduced fee.

• Mary Ann graduated from a two-year associate degree nursing program. Since she had always enjoyed traveling and found the regular routine of a nine-to-five job tiresome, she was very excited when her nursing advisor suggested that she explore job opportunities as a ship nurse for large passenger ship lines. She became a temporary ship nurse for two firms and has made three voyages as one of three nurses assisting the ship physician. Currently she is enrolled in a bachelor's-to-master's degree program leading to the role of family nurse practitioner. Mary Ann has requested a permanent position as a practitioner with one particular ship line and hopes that her request will be granted shortly. Her job responsibilities so far have included teaching passengers how to avoid overexposure to the sun, preventing or subduing seasickness, and helping to set a passenger's fractured arm—the result of an exuberant volleyball game.

• Debbi is an R.N. who received a bachelor's degree in nursing, worked in a community health center, and recently earned a master's degree in community health nursing. Following graduation, she and another nurse, whose master's degree is in medical and surgical nursing, opened a private nursing practice as independent practitioners in their local community. At this time, the practice is only a part-time venture, and they each hold a regular part-time position to support themselves financially until the nursing practice expands. On a typical day, Debbi visits three clients and administers intravenous antibiotics (based on a physician's order) to treat Lyme disease; teaches a newly diagnosed diabetic about diet, skin care, and insulin administration; and counsels an elderly woman on coping with her bedridden husband. One evening a week, Debbi and her associate assist a group of overweight clients, focusing on improving self-esteem, body image, and nutritional habits.

• Although Marcella had a baccalaureate degree in economics, she was always interested in the health field and finally concluded that nursing would be an ideal profession. It provided job security, career mobility, benefits, and flexibility in hours (full-time, part-time, flextime). Nursing allowed her to be employed part-time and manage her children, husband, and home. Currently she is an R.N. and a graduate student in an adult-health, clinical-nurse specialist program.

Nursing Ethics

Nurses, as providers of human services, participate in providing comprehensive health care. They often function as members of health care teams. As team members and as professionals, they are accountable for their actions.

It is difficult to define ethics. Essentially, ethics are the guidelines used to judge whether an act is right or wrong. The American Nurses Association Code for Nurses, first published in 1950, was revised in 1985 and again in 2001 by the ANA. It includes the following nine provisions, which influence decisions made by nurses that affect the quality of patient care and, ultimately, the nursing profession:

1. The nurse, in all professional relationships, practices with compassion and respect for the inherent dignity, worth, and uniqueness of every individual, unrestricted by considerations of social or economic status, personal attributes, or the nature of health problems.
2. The nurse's primary commitment is to the patient, whether an individual, family, group, or community.
3. The nurse promotes, advocates for, and strives to protect the health, safety, and rights of the patient.
4. The nurse is responsible and accountable for individual nursing practice and determines the appropriate delegation of tasks consistent with the nurse's obligation to provide optimum patient care.
5. The nurse owes the same duties to self as to others, including the responsibility to preserve integrity and safety, to maintain competence, and to continue personal and professional growth.

6. The nurse participates in establishing, maintaining, and improving health care environments and conditions of employment conducive to the provision of quality health care and consistent with the values of the profession through individual and collective action.

7. The nurse participates in the advancement of the profession through contributions to practice, education, administration, and knowledge development.

8. The nurse collaborates with other health professionals and the public in promoting community, national, and international efforts to meet health needs.

9. The profession of nursing, as represented by associations and their members, is responsible for articulating nursing values, for maintaining the integrity of the profession and its practice, and for shaping social policy.

The International Council of Nurses, Code of Ethics for Nurses, was revised in 2000. It has four principal elements that outline the standards of ethical conduct. They are summarized here:

Nurses and People

The nurse's primary professional responsibility is to people who require nursing care.

In providing care, the nurse promotes an environment in which the human rights, values, customs, and spiritual beliefs of the individual, family, and community are respected.

The nurse ensures that the individual receives sufficient information on which to base consent for care and related treatment.

The nurse holds in confidence personal information and uses judgment sharing this information.

The nurse shares with society the responsibility for initiating and supporting action to meet the health and social needs of the public, in particular those of vulnerable populations.

The nurse also shares responsibility to sustain and protect the natural environment from depletion, pollution, degradation, and destruction.

Nurses and Practice

The nurse carries personal responsibility and accountability for nursing practice and for maintaining competence by continual learning.

The nurse maintains a standard of personal health such that the ability to provide care is not compromised.

The nurse uses judgment regarding individual competence when accepting and delegating responsibility.

The nurse at all times maintains standards of personal conduct that reflect well on the profession and enhance public confidence.

The nurse, in providing care, ensures that use of technology and scientific advances are compatible with the safety, dignity, and rights of people.

Nurses and the Profession

The nurse assumes the major role in determining and implementing acceptable standards of clinical nursing practice, management, research, and education.

The nurse is active in developing a core of research-based professional knowledge.

The nurse, acting through the professional organization, participates in creating and maintaining equitable social and economic working conditions in nursing.

Nurses and Coworkers

The nurse sustains a cooperative relationship with coworkers in nursing and other fields.

The nurse takes appropriate action to safeguard individuals when a coworker or any other person endangers their care.

It should be noted that, according to the ANA code, nurses are responsible for all of their actions. They must be knowledgeable and informed about all decisions when involved with patient care. For example, when nurses administer medication to patients, they are just as responsible for incorrect dosages as the physicians who prescribe them. Therefore, nurses must know the average dose of a drug, its actions, side effects, and what dosages are considered to be excessive.

Another area that is assuming more importance is the ethical responsibility of the nurse engaged in or conducting research. The nurse who is assisting in unethical research is just as responsible as the individual who designs it. For example, research is considered unethical if its subjects are not informed that they are being exposed to a disease that is life-threatening or might cause permanent damage if untreated. The nurse who merely records the blood pressure of those subjects is considered just as unethical as the individual who conducts the study.

Nurses must act on their own ethical convictions; however, in accordance with the code, they perform as a part of the total occupational group of nursing.

In the following chapter, we will explore, in detail, the duties of each member of the health care team, nursing career paths, and attributes necessary to succeed in the field.

2

NURSING TODAY

THE PROVISION OF health care in the United States is a complex, often frustrating task. Health care is provided by approximately forty thousand facilities, such as community health centers, hospitals, clinics, and nursing homes. There are approximately 4.5 million workers functioning within fifty different categories; however, since this is the age of specialization, such categories can be further dissected into job titles. According to the National Institutes of Health, Bureau of Health Manpower Education, there are more than 250 job descriptions for health personnel. The number and complexity of job titles is confusing both to patients and students preparing for positions in the health care field. To add to the confusion, job titles often vary geographically and even from one institution to another within the same city. For example, the individual who answers the phone, takes care of ordering supplies, and attends to administrative details may be called a ward clerk, ward secretary, ward receptionist, or even some other job title. To alleviate this difficulty with job titles, most health care facilities maintain a notebook with job descriptions for all personnel.

The Health Care Team

The health care team may be composed of a variety of personnel, depending on the setting, the needs of the patients, the financial resources for hiring personnel, and the preparation and qualifications of the team members. In a moderate-sized hospital, a typical health care team might consist of a professional nurse, physician, physical therapist, occupational therapist, dietitian, social worker, and pharmacist. This team may vary according to the members available and the needs of individual patients. Each member of the health care team contributes specific knowledge and skills to patient care. Most members have completed a specified amount of education, and a few are licensed specifically to provide their services. A description of the services individual members provide may help you to better understand the team.

Nurse

The nursing staff is composed of a variety of workers plus many more who function under the supervision of the nurse. The nursing staff in a hospital usually consists of the nursing director, a nursing supervisor, a nurse manager, advanced practice nurses (such as nurse practitioners and clinical nurse specialists), and the floor nurses, who are a mixture of registered and licensed practical nurses (L.P.N.). The L.P.N. is licensed to provide patient care under the supervision of the registered nurse (R.N.). Because of differences in educational preparation, the professional R.N. is expected to handle more complex cases and with more expertise, in addition to supervising subordinates.

The nurses' aides, orderlies, nursing assistants, and nursing care technicians provide basic patient care and related services under the supervision of the professional nurse. A typical assignment might be to help bathe the patient and change the linen, give out trays for the unit, collect and package patient unit supplies, take temperatures, weigh patients, and ready units for new patient admissions. In addition, many institutions have a preliminary training program in which nursing assistants learn how to take temperature, blood pressure, and pulse readings.

Ward receptionists or ward clerks are also under the supervision of the nurse. Typical responsibilities include preparing patient charts, ordering ward supplies, greeting new patients and completing initial patient processing, answering the phone, and scheduling various procedures and tests.

Physician

The physician is responsible for the diagnosis and treatment of disease and for the patient's therapeutic medical regimen. The medical doctor is the head of the medical health care team. In some institutions or settings, other members of the health team assume the position of head of the overall health care team.

The physician's education usually consists of three or four years of college, four years of medical school, and, for specialization, from two to five years of internship and residency experience. Recently medical school education has been stressing a comprehensive and humanistic approach, emphasizing areas such as family practice medicine and community health medicine.

To keep up with the increasing demands on the physician, a new specialty area has appeared under the title of the physician assistant (P.A.). Many P.A.s qualify for their jobs by completing four years of college plus a training period. The physician assistant functions under the supervision of the physician and usually performs duties that include administering routine physical examinations, carrying out standard procedures such as laboratory work and suturing, and assisting the physician with routine tasks and procedures.

Physical Therapist

The physical therapist is responsible for restoring and maintaining mobility when disease or injury has resulted in loss or altered function of a body part. Physical therapists utilize techniques such as exercise, tilt tables, the application of heat and cold, and training in the use of crutches.

Occupational Therapist

The primary responsibility of the occupational therapist is to promote and maintain patient functions that relate in particular to the activities of daily living. This may include treatment designed to alter or enhance a patient's vocational skills or abilities required for dressing, cooking, and grooming. The occupational therapist usually has a baccalaureate degree that includes special courses and experience in occupational therapy.

Dietitian

The dietitian is responsible for the selection of food appropriate to the patient's medical and hospital regimen. Sometimes nutritional teaching and menu alteration according to individual needs are part of the dietitian's job. Dietitians usually complete a baccalaureate degree and an internship.

Social Worker

The social worker provides assistance to the client through contacts with community and other social agencies that offer specific resources. The social worker's focus is on clients and their families and how the patients' illnesses or hospitalization affect their families. The social worker usually has a baccalaureate degree, and many positions in social work require that the individual also have a master's degree in social work.

Pharmacist

The pharmacist is a licensed professional who has completed approximately five years of education that usually include two years of specialized education in a school of pharmacy. It is the pharmacist's responsibility to mix and/or dispense medications. The pharmacist also advises the health care team about the actions and side effects of the drugs the patient is receiving and often serves as a consultant to the physician regarding new medications and the advisability and effects of mixing medications.

The list of other health care team members is endless, but a sampling of the various areas of responsibility might illustrate the extent of services the patient receives either directly or indirectly. The list includes the speech pathologist, kidney dialysis technician, dental assistant, various types of radiologists, surgical technician, music therapist, optician, and the psychologist.

It would be impossible for a health care facility to hire and utilize someone from each care field, even though the specialized services of various occupations may be required. In such cases a mixing of roles usually occurs, with some occupations engaging in a wide range of activities. For example, it is conceivable that the nurse may perform some functions that seem more closely related to the duties of a dietitian, social worker, recreational therapist, or inhalation therapist.

A good example is the case of one Mrs. Smith. Recently Mrs. Smith experienced an episode of dizziness, severe headache, and brief loss of consciousness. When she regained consciousness, she noted some difficulty with her speech and a weakness and slight paralysis of her left arm and leg. Mr. Smith phoned their doctor, Dr. Jones, who hospitalized Mrs. Smith immediately. The Smiths arrived at the hospital where the admitting clerk filled out the admission forms and assigned Mrs. Smith to a room as an emergency admission. Mrs. Smith, accompanied by her husband, was escorted in a wheelchair to the fourth floor by the admission desk porter. Once on the fourth floor, the ward secretary greeted the Smiths, and Mrs. Smith was given a wristband stamped with her name and unit number. The nurse team leader then escorted Mrs. Smith to her room, asking Mr. Smith to wait in the visitor's room. With the nursing assistant, the team leader helped Mrs. Smith into a hospital gown; measured and recorded routine blood pressure, temperature, and pulse data; and, with Mr. Smith in the room, completed an admission interview. (The team leader also records the health history and makes a tentative nursing diagnosis.)

Mrs. Smith's physician had notified the floor staff of her admission and ordered a number of tests performed. Following the admission, the transporter arrived, placed Mrs. Smith on the stretcher, and wheeled her to the x-ray department. Several x-ray examinations were done by an x-ray technician and a radiologist (a physician). After she returned to her room, a dietitian arrived to help Mrs. Smith fill out her menu. The dietitian noted that Mrs. Smith had a preference for fish and disliked spicy and fried foods. A number of blood samples were drawn by the laboratory technician and analyzed immediately to assist Dr. Jones in completing a diagnosis.

Dr. Jones, making rounds, greets Mrs. Smith and tells her that the results of the tests are in and that, following an examination, she will be given a medical diagnosis. The complete examination, which included neurological tests for nerve functioning, is over, and Dr. Jones informs the Smiths that the patient has experienced a mild cerebrovascular accident, better known as a stroke. The physician also advises them of the rehabilitation and treatment plan.

During her hospital stay, many health care personnel treat Mrs. Smith. Once a day she works out with a physical therapist to restore function to her left leg and arm. She has daily sessions with an occupational therapist who teaches her to weave, an activity that will strengthen the muscles in her left arm and fingers. A speech therapist works with Mrs. Smith to restore her speech and reduce slurring. During this rehabilitation period, Mrs. Smith also comes into contact with the social worker, who begins planning for such things as the financial assistance for installing grab bars in the Smiths' bathroom at home. Others who work with Mrs. Smith include a pharmacist; an orthotist, who measures her for a short leg brace to provide added support for her left leg; and the psychometrician, who gives her a battery of mental and psychological tests to determine to what extent Mrs. Smith's thinking and emotional processes have been damaged by the stroke.

As the time for discharge draws near, the team nurse working with Mrs. Smith completes a referral form recommending that a visiting nurse make home visits weekly to the Smiths.

From this you can see that Mrs. Smith's recovery is assisted by the activities of a variety of health care workers, all of whom communicate with one another.

Nursing Shortage and Demand

Consider the duties of the student nurse in 1855. Nurses were required to be:

- sober
- honest
- truthful
- trustworthy
- quiet/orderly
- clean/neat
- patient/cheerful/kindly
- punctual

Nurses were expected to become skillful in:

- dressing blisters, burns, sores, and wounds and applying fomentations, poultices, and minor dressings
- applying leeches, externally and internally
- administering enemas for men and women
- managing trusses and appliances of uterine complaints
- using the best method of friction to the body and to extremities

- managing helpless patients—moving, changing, personal
  cleanliness of, feeding, keeping warm, preventing and dressing bedsores, managing position of
- bandaging, making bandages and rollers, and lining splints
- making beds and removing sheets while patients were still
  in bed
- attending operations
- cooking gruel, arrowroot, egg flip, and puddings, and providing drinks for the sick
- understanding ventilation, or keeping the ward fresh by
  night as well as day
- being careful that great cleanliness was observed in all
  utensils—those used for secretions as well as for cooking
- making strict observations of the sick in the following par-
  ticulars: secretions, expectoration, pulse, skin, appetite,
  intelligence, delirium or stupor, breathing, sleep, state of
  wounds, eruptions, formation of matter, effect of diet,
  effect of stimulants and of medicine
- learning the management of convalescents

In addition to the above duties, nurses in the late 1800s and
early 1900s were expected to work exceptionally long hours for very
low pay. It was not unusual for nurses to spend twelve hours a day,
six days a week caring for the sick, and earning only enough money
to pay their rent and buy food. If there happened to be any money
left over, nurses were expected to contribute the remainder to char-
ity. Yet, in spite of the poor rewards, hard work, and low status,
many young women sought nursing as a career.

Historically there has always been a nursing shortage, and today
in most regions there still are not sufficient numbers of properly

prepared nurses to meet the ever-changing demands. A number of government reports and privately funded and nonfunded research studies have attributed the current inadequate supply to:

- incompatibility between the educational experience and the pressure and demands experienced by the neophyte staff nurse
- lack of reward for educational differences and for bedside care
- low salaries
- ineffective utilization of nurses already employed
- poor professional image that discourages higher-quality college-bound students

Recent surveys of the issues that contribute to the nursing shortage point to more than just salary as a source of dissatisfaction. Among some of the major dissatisfactions are the unavailability of child care facilities, lack of support from hospital administrators, large amount of paperwork done by nursing staff, lack of support from nurse administrators, unavailability of help when a patient needs extra care, R.N.-to-patient ratio, availability of continuing education opportunities, and availability of in-service education. In addition, sexual stereotypes of nurses do not provide an accurate picture of contemporary nursing practice.

The goal of the health care system is to expand nursing practice. This ongoing goal will create increasing opportunities for nurses to take a leading role in the delivery of primary care. More nurses are enhancing their careers by becoming nurse anesthetists, nurse-midwives, nurse practitioners, and clinical nurse specialists. The future of nursing practice will expand to include outpatient, ambulatory, community, and long-term settings. Advances in technology will change the record-keeping and documentation practices of nurses. New technology will broaden the knowledge base, facilitate decision-making, and increase access to scientific information upon which to base nursing practice.

As the need for improved health care continues and the roles and responsibilities of nurses become more complex and specialized, there will be an ever-increasing demand for nurses with more education related to primary care, education, and management. A report called "2000 Registered Nurse Population: Findings from the National Sample of Registered Nurses" indicates that the job market for registered nurses in general is expected to rise much faster than the average for all occupations in response to the health care needs of a growing and aging population. Agencies and health care settings in many of the larger metropolitan areas offer higher pay. The need for registered nurses is greater than for many other occupations due to the expansion of the nurse's role in hospitals and ambulatory care settings, the increased emphasis on health promotion, and the need to fill the vacancies created by nurses who leave nursing. With the extension and expansion of nurses' roles, there is an opportunity to reduce the escalating health care costs now facing insurance companies and American consumers as well. Nurses with graduate degrees are in very high demand in any area or setting.

The Bureau of Labor Statistics estimates that about 50 percent of the job openings in the health care occupations between 1988 and 1998 were for nursing personnel.

Another consideration is the continued need for nurses who are better prepared. The educational preparation of today's nurse is hardly comparable to that of even twenty-five years ago. The following table shows, by percent, the educational preparation of practicing nurses in five sample years:

Highest Academic Credentials of Registered Nurses Practicing in the United States—1964, 1974, 1986, 1992, and 2000

	Ph.D./M.A.	B.A./B.S.	N.D.*	A.A.
1964	2.3%	9.0%	88.7%	NA
1974	3.3	15.2	75.5	6.0%
1986	5.6	25.5	45.3	23.6
1992	7.3	32.0	32.5	28.2
2000	8.9	36.1	35.5	19.5

*Nursing Diploma

Source: *Source Book, Nursing Personnel*. DHEW Publication No. (HRA) 75-43, U.S. Department of Health, Education, and Welfare Public Health Service

From this table it becomes apparent that the trend is for practicing nurses to seek education from schools within a college or university setting and to seek higher levels of educational preparation.

Thus nursing offers excellent prospects for employment and diversity of employment. For nurses who have children in particular, the opportunity for employment in a variety of settings on either a full- or part-time basis is a distinct advantage. The possibility of arranging flexible hours makes nursing a career that can easily be worked into the needs and schedule of a family.

In a few instances, however, this may not be the case, depending on the geographical location. Consistent with other occupations, the supply and demand of nursing personnel may vary greatly according to the section of the country, and there may be few opportunities to schedule work according to personal schedule preferences.

Presently there is an increased demand for nurses nationwide. According to a joint study by the Department of Health and Human Services and the Centers for Disease Control, the educational levels attained by active nursing personnel practicing in the United States in roughly the last twenty years are as follows:

Education of Nursing Personnel

	1980	1985	1990	1995	1998
R.N.	560,000	641,400	713,700	797,600	828,400
A.A. and Nursing					
Diploma	399,900	425,800	441,600	465,500	473,900
B.A.	130,900	175,600	218,900	253,800	268,200
M.A. and Ph.D.	29,600	39,900	53,200	78,200	86,400

One thing is certain from the national point of view. There is now, and will be for the indefinite future, a greater demand than supply of nurses, particularly the professionally educated nurse. This is based on two factors: the number of available positions paying salaries that are acceptable, and the needs of the people, as determined both by the public and by the profession.

Job Satisfaction

Nursing is a rewarding career in many ways. It offers job satisfaction within a variety of settings that may be changed according to personal needs and interests. Nursing offers the opportunity for giving assistance and services to people who need help. For example, a public health nurse in New York City experiences a feeling of satisfaction after administering an injection to an elderly woman and spending time with her to alleviate her loneliness. Or consider the feelings of a surgical nurse in a pediatric unit who explains hernia surgery to an anxious child. After the two of them "operate" on a surgical doll, he looks up, smiles, and says, "Gee, nurse, I feel better."

Nurses can observe the results of their labor within a fairly short time. Unlike the scientist or research chemist, whose work on a discovery of a new plastic may take six to eight months or longer, the nurse observes the patient's relief within twenty minutes following the administration of a pain medicine. Marilyn, an industrial nurse in a large company, discusses the enjoyment she receives from her job: "If I provide relief from pain or treat an employee's stress reaction, workers always return within a few days to say thanks for helping when they really needed it."

As an integral part of the health care team, a nurse has an opportunity to make a unique contribution. It is the nursing staff in a hospital setting that observes and provides care to patients for the total twenty-four-hour period. The nurse is, therefore, in the very unusual position of knowing how and when a patient responds to treatment, medications, or personal relations throughout the entire day/night cycle. Rita, the charge nurse for a cardiac intensive care unit, tells with great enthusiasm about the rewards of her position: "I'm here five days a week, for seven to eight hours a day. It is just such an exciting job, working with the patients, receiving the training, monitoring and interpreting the cardiac strips, and using these tools for making nursing decisions. I guess what I like most is the feeling that my contribution to the patient's care and recovery is as important as that of anyone else on the team. For example, last week a patient was having all kinds of irregular beats, in spite of his medication. On rounds I told the physician that the patient was anxious and worried. As a result of our spending extra time with him so he could tell us his feelings, that patient's rhythm strip looks much better now."

Expanded educational opportunities and increased flexibility and variety in the roles nurses now assume have made nursing more and more attractive and have resulted in more men entering the field. The number of male nursing applicants and graduates is increasing. George, a former army medic, is now completing his associate degree in nursing. He says he selected nursing for many reasons, but two in particular headed his list: "I have a wife and a two-year-old child to support. At the community college, I take most of my liberal arts classes in the evening so I can work downtown during the day. I like working with people and nursing is good for me. It offers so many challenging job opportunities that are stable. I can be a clinician in just about any unit at the hospital, and the starting salary is good."

Nursing offers a variety of educational routes, depending on a student's interests, goals, capabilities, and finances. In addition, the educational system provides a good foundation in both knowledge and skills that prepare the student for employment and, in some cases, for future additional educational preparation. There are probably few other fields where the variety of roles one may assume is as diverse and varied as nursing. Mary, age forty-nine, has a doctorate in nursing and is currently the dean of nursing at a major university. She says of her career: "Nursing was the most appropriate field for me. I completed a bachelor's degree in nursing, then worked as a staff nurse on a neurological and rehabilitation floor. As my interests developed, I took a head nurse position on an ophthalmological (eye) unit. Soon I discovered my challenges and rewards came from teaching and instructing, so I completed a master's degree in nursing. The rewards of the teaching job that followed the master's degree were very satisfying. However, new questions and challenges made me realize the need for more education, particularly to learn how to carry out responsible research. Since I completed my doctorate, I have been able to teach, practice, and do research. Now I'm in administration, although I continue teaching a course, care for a few patients, and direct a research grant. No other profession would have allowed me the flexibility to pursue my interests within such a wide range."

Claudette, age thirty-eight, began her career as a nurse's aide when she was divorced with two small children. She earned an L.P.N., an associate degree in nursing, and a baccalaureate degree. She worked nights, raised the children, and then returned to school for her master's degree in the family nurse practitioner program. She now earns $70,000 a year working in a large health maintenance organization. She works nine to five, five days a week, and her eyes light up as she talks about her work. "I see a steady group of patients and families and get to know them over time. I do their history and physical and see them for the usual problems like ear infections, sinusitis, and allergies. I just love what I do and plan to take some more courses, like shiatsu and family therapy, which will help me with my work."

The field of nursing is probably in one of its most exciting eras. Involvement in nursing at this time offers the challenge—and the frustration—of a profession that is forging ahead to assert its independence and sense of identity. The state nurses association hired Helen to represent it as its state lobbyist on legislative issues affecting nurses and nursing practice. "Frankly," she says, "the politico-legal scene is really where it's at. If nurses want autonomy and an identity, it must come from the legal arena and be protected through political know-how."

Salaries

Professional challenge and personal job satisfaction are only two factors that make nursing an exciting and rewarding field.

Salaries, too, offer tangible rewards and are constantly improving, with the result that nurses are in a far better position financially than they were just ten years ago. This improvement is in part the result of nurses demanding fair payment for their services.

It is also, in part, a result of the initiation and implementation of collective bargaining with unions or associations being paid to represent nursing and the interests of individual nurses at the bargaining table with management. The median annual salary of registered nurses in 2000 was $44,840.

Consequently, a new graduate with an associate degree or a degree from a hospital nursing school who has passed the licensing examination should expect a beginning salary of approximately $24.49 per hour. The specific salary figure is set by the hiring agency and is affected by geographical location. In addition, most nurses now enjoy fringe benefits such as paid vacations, holiday time, tuition, reimbursement plans, and health insurance. Nurses graduating with baccalaureate or graduate degrees can expect slightly higher starting salaries than nurses with associate degrees or nursing diplomas; those with doctorates should expect even more. With additional experience and/or education, nurses assume positions in administration, clinical specialties, and education, with salaries correspondingly higher. For example, a nurse with a Ph.D. may earn $150,000 a year as an administrator in a hospital, or a nurse with a master's degree teaching in a private college may earn $50,000 to $60,000 a year.

A new practical nurse who has graduated and passed the licensing examination may expect to earn about $35,000 per year ($10.98 to $15.87 per hour). Again, this salary varies according to the institution and geographic location.

Attributes Necessary for Nursing

There are several requirements necessary to succeed in the field of nursing. These requirements—physical, emotional, intellectual, and economic—are discussed below.

Physical Requirements

The U.S. Bureau of Health Professions, Division of Nursing, states that the nursing workforce is aging. The average age of graduates from nursing programs is thirty-two. The average age of practicing R.N.s is forty-four. Nursing requires good physical and mental health. The degree of physical stamina required may vary depending on the specialty area. However, most nursing positions, with the exception of psychiatric nursing, require assisting patients in activities of daily living, which may include lifting and turning heavy patients. The individual who finds utilizing physical strength over a period of time a problem would probably prefer an outpatient well-baby clinic.

Those with very minor physical limitations might find nursing to be a suitable career. However, individuals who require major appliances for mobility, such as wheelchairs or long leg braces, might not be as able to meet the physical demands placed on nurses.

Emotional Requirements

The major emotional attributes required for success in nursing are desire and ability to deal with people. Nursing is truly a people-oriented profession, and many of its skills are based on interpersonal techniques. Therefore, the individual who finds people uninteresting or prefers to be alone should not consider nursing.

Another emotional attribute that is helpful is empathy. Empathy is the ability to respond to another person with a feeling of knowing what he or she is experiencing. This does not imply that nurses should be so grief-stricken over a patient's death that they are ineffective in dealing with the surviving family. Skilled nurses communicate an appropriate amount of sadness to family members, then assist them during the mourning period.

Intellectual Requirements

Because of the increase in nursing school applications and reductions in admission, some schools have become more selective. Most schools admit students according to their prior academic record and recommendations from teachers and instructors concerning their future academic potential. Therefore it is advisable for students who are interested in a nursing career to make academic performance in high school a priority. Schools of nursing within a college or university set up admission criteria consistent with the rest of the institution. Most baccalaureate programs require certain minimum scores on the Scholastic Aptitude Test (SAT); others use the National League for Nursing's Prenursing Test Battery.

Economic Requirements

The initial financial outlay for an education in nursing may vary greatly, according to the route taken. The variation is from little or no tuition at a school for practical nursing to almost $7,500 a year or more at a baccalaureate degree program within a private college or university setting.

Other costs to consider are room and board or living expenses, uniforms, books, various laboratory and student activity fees, and transportation costs to and from classroom and clinical laboratory settings. These can bring the total to as high as $50,000 in some schools.

Financial assistance is available from various health institutions in the form of loans, grants, and scholarships. A list of addresses to write to for further information about assistance can be found in Chapter 3.

3

CHOOSING THE RIGHT EDUCATIONAL ROUTE

TODAY FORMAL EDUCATION in nursing is required before a person is legally qualified to practice and be called a nurse. The educational route a student takes depends upon his or her goals, career objectives, and scholastic ability.

There are currently three avenues of nursing preparation: hospital schools of nursing, whose graduates are eligible for the registered nurse (R.N.) examination; schools offering the associate degree; and schools for practical nursing, whose graduates are eligible for the licensed practical nurse (L.P.N.) or licensed vocational nurse (L.V.N.) examination. Graduates who have earned baccalaureate degrees are eligible to take the R.N. licensure examination after completion of their program.

Although the preparation routes may differ, there are some common traits among them that represent changes in nursing education policy over the past ten or more years. For example, many schools offer dormitory-style living facilities, many mixed with students from other disciplines such as liberal arts or dental hygiene. However, most students are also given the option of living off campus or commuting.

The characteristics of students in nursing classes have changed, too. Students now come from both sexes, from different age groups (particularly older ones), and from many cultures.

Registered Nurse Programs: The Hospital School

The registered nurse (R.N.) provides nursing care to patients and their families in a variety of health care settings. One educational route that provides this preparation is a hospital program in nursing; however, these programs are is declining dramatically. Education in higher-education institutions is rising significantly and is often cited as the preferred route for many employers.

The individual who completes a hospital program is eligible for the registered nurse licensure examination and is prepared to function as a generalist in such health care settings as hospitals and other community institutions. The hospital-school graduate "provides nursing care and engages in therapeutic, rehabilitative, and preventive activities in behalf of individual patients and groups of patients," according to the National League for Nursing. The hospital program is best suited for the student who is interested in an education primarily within a hospital setting where patient contact begins early and is continuous throughout the experience.

Educational preparation for the student utilizing the hospital-school route generally requires twenty-four to thirty months and is usually set up within three calendar years. Most hospital schools do require full-time study, although there might be some allowance for a part-time job.

The hospital nursing program is offered through a hospital or, in a few cases, through an independently incorporated group. Although the current trend is away from hospital-school education, since the inception of formalized education for nurses, it has been hospital-school education that has provided the bulk of the nurses practicing today. The shift toward baccalaureate and associate degree nursing preparation and away from hospital-school education may in some way be attributed to students' desire for college-based education, to the reluctance of hospitals to absorb increasing costs for educating students, and to the nursing profession's desire to place nursing education under the guidance of institutions of higher learning rather than under the administration of the hospital itself.

Tuition costs for hospital schools of nursing are approximately $3,500 in public settings and $5,200 in private schools. However, tuition is usually reduced with each year of education. In addition, there are expenses for room, board, and other related living costs, such as textbooks and other materials. In a few schools these fees are included in the total bill.

Entrance requirements include graduation from high school or its equivalent with satisfactory academic performance in a college preparatory program and good mental and physical health.

The course of study in a hospital nursing school consists of such courses as the theory and practice of medical-surgical, maternal-child, or psychiatric nursing. In addition, many schools require students to take courses in the physical, biological, and social sciences. A typical course of study might look like this:

First Year

First Semester	Second Semester
Nursing Fundamentals	Medical-Surgical Nursing
Anatomy and Physiology	Pathophysiology
Microbiology	Expository Writing
Introduction to Psychology	

Second Year

First Semester	Second Semester
Maternity-Pediatric Nursing	Psych/Mental Health Nursing
Child Psychology	Sociology
	Community Health

Third Year

First Semester	Second Semester
Medical-Surgical Nursing II	Leadership in Nursing
Cultural Anthropology	Nursing Trends

In some hospital programs, students no longer put in the customary long hours of hospital service, nor do they staff the hospital's evening or night shifts. Students may work an evening or night shift, often accompanied by the instructor.

Upon successful completion of the diploma nursing program, the graduate is permitted to take the state licensure examination. Individuals who score passing marks on this exam are then legally permitted to sign their name followed by the initials R.N. and can practice nursing under the title of registered nurse in the state that issued the license.

Career advancement for the hospital-prepared registered nurse is possible, but it is important to note that many positions of advancement beyond the diploma preparation may require a master's degree in nursing. In fact, a number of hospitals within the large metropolitan areas are hiring nurses with a minimum of baccalaureate preparation. Since nursing educators have identified differences in the depth and scope of knowledge between hospital and baccalaureate education, hospital graduates are required to register for many nursing courses that may include repeated content; however, the approach and level of content will be different. The trend is to recognize and give credit for previously learned knowledge through the use of proficiency exams, equivalency testing, and content challenge exams. In addition, there are a number of baccalaureate degree nursing programs designed specifically for the diplomate R.N. who wishes to earn a B.S. in nursing. This usually requires two calendar years and possibly extra time to complete any additional liberal arts requirements.

Technical Registered Nurse Programs: The Associate Degree

The individual who completes an associate degree program in nursing is then also eligible for the registered nurse licensure examination. As an R.N., a nurse is qualified to plan and provide care for individuals and their families in such health care settings as nursing homes and hospitals.

The associate degree program in nursing was developed in 1952 by Dr. Mildred Montag, a nurse and educator. Her idea resulted from a need to prepare a nurse who would be skilled in providing excellent bedside care with a broad knowledge and judgment base. However, the associate degree graduate was not originally intended to assume leadership or administrative roles. According to Montag, the functions of the associate degree nurse are to assist with planning nursing care, provide general nursing care with supervision, and assist with the evaluation of nursing care. Essentially, the role of the associate degree nurse has been described as providing nurse care in specific, prescribed nursing situations and planning and providing care in more complex situations in conjunction with a professional nurse.

The associate degree program is best suited for the student who is interested in a community-based program leading to eligibility to become licensed as an R.N. The program leads to a college degree; an A.A. or A.A.S. degree in nursing may be completed in a relatively short period, varying from two calendar years to two academic years. Consistent with a college course of study, the associate degree in nursing may be pursued on a part-time basis, particularly during the completion of the college course. However, most of the nursing courses require nearly full-time study.

Associate degree programs are offered through public junior community colleges, private institutions, senior colleges or universities, or technical institutes. Most programs are conducted within community or junior colleges. The current trend is toward preparation of nurses in college or university settings and away from hospital-school preparation.

The tuition and living expenses for nursing students are very similar to those of other students within the community college system. The expenses are less for students whose permanent residence is in the same community, since community colleges allow a sizable tuition reduction for residents. There is also a decided financial advantage to living at home rather than in a dormitory.

Requirements for admission to an associate degree program may vary from an open admission policy in a city community system to fairly strict policies requiring high scores on the SAT for a private junior college. It is safe to assume that all programs require graduation from high school and a good academic record. In planning for admission to an associate degree program in nursing, it is wise to obtain the school catalog or bulletin early to learn about admission criteria.

The course of study in an associate degree nursing school consists of study almost equally divided between nursing education and college-level general education. Students in the nursing program attend the same classes for their supportive (non-nursing) subjects, as do other students in the college. Many prospective students find this a particularly positive experience. It allows for an integration of ideas between nursing and other disciplines, thus providing a more expansive college experience.

A typical course of study in an associate degree program might be planned as follows:

First Year

First Semester
Introduction to
  Nursing Concepts
English
Introduction to Psychology
Anatomy and Physiology I

Second Semester
Application of
  Nursing Concepts
English II
Anatomy and Physiology II

Second Year

First Semester
Nursing and Physical
  Needs I
Nursing and Emotional
  Needs, Nursing Concepts
Introduction to Microbiology
Sociology

Second Semester
Nursing and Physical
  Needs II
Philosophy
Liberal Arts Elective

The typical schedule might require attendance at a nursing clinical laboratory in a local hospital twice a week for eight hours, two credit hours of nursing theory class for four hours a week, and three to six hours of college courses a week. Students in the associate degree program use the clinical laboratory (formerly known as hospital experience) as a place to test out nursing theory learned in class and to explore the different roles a nurse assumes in the course of performing his or her duties. In addition, most nursing programs use a college laboratory (a classroom for practicing nursing skills) to teach students nursing skills, such as blood pressure measurement and bandaging, prior to their performance of such tasks on real patients.

After successfully completing the associate degree nursing program, the graduate is prepared to take the state R.N. licensure examination. Individuals who score passing marks are then permitted by license to practice nursing in the state where the exam was passed. They are also authorized to use the initials R.N. when signing their names.

It is very important when selecting an educational program in nursing to remember that the associate degree program is considered a terminal program; that is, upon completion, the graduate has been prepared to pursue a career essentially as a staff nurse. If the associate degree graduate wishes to pursue a baccalaureate degree, some of the credits may not be applicable. On the other hand, some baccalaureate degree programs are designed to expedite the completion of a higher degree, requiring approximately two years for an R.N. with an associate degree to earn a baccalaureate degree in nursing. Graduating high school students with aspirations for bachelor's degrees and/or leadership positions in nursing should be encouraged not to pursue the associate degree route but to select a baccalaureate nursing program.

Licensed Practical Nurses and Licensed Vocational Nurses

The licensed practical nurse or licensed vocational nurse may work under the supervision of a registered nurse or a physician, providing nursing care in uncomplicated situations. In cases requiring more complex care, the role of the practical or vocational nurse is to act as the registered nurse's assistant.

Functions

The national organization for practical nurses, the National Federation of Licensed Practical Nurses, states that the function of the practical nurse acting under the supervision of a registered nurse and/or physician is to assist with the planning, implementation, and evaluation of patient care by:

1. Providing for the emotional and physical comfort and safety of patients through
   a. the understanding of human relationships between and among patients, families, and other health care personnel;
   b. participation in the development, revision, and implementation of policies and procedures designed to ensure comfort and safety of patients and other health care personnel;
   c. assisting the patient with activities of daily living and encouraging appropriate self-care;
   d. recognizing and understanding the effects of social and economic problems upon patients;
   e. protecting patients from behavior that would damage their self-esteem or relationship with families, other patients, or persons;
   f. recognizing and understanding cultural backgrounds and spiritual needs and respecting the religious beliefs of individual patients; and
   g. considering needs of the patient for an attractive, comfortable, and safe environment.

2. Observing, recording, and reporting to the appropriate persons
   a. general and specific physical and mental conditions of patients, and signs and symptoms that may be indicative of change; and
   b. stresses in human relationships between patients, patients' families, visitors, and health care personnel.
3. Performing more specialized nursing functions for which the L.P.N. is prepared, such as
   a. administration of medications and therapeutic treatments prescribed for the patient;
   b. preparation and care of patients receiving specialized treatments; and
   c. carrying out first-aid, emergency, and disaster measures.
4. Assisting with rehabilitation of patients, according to the patient care plan, through
   a. knowledge and application of the principles of prevention of deformities (for example, the normal range of motion exercises, body mechanics, and alignments);
   b. encouragement of patients to help themselves within their own capabilities;
   c. awareness of and encouraging the fulfillment of the special aptitudes and interests of patients; and
   d. utilizing community resources and facilities for continuing patient care.

Education

The education for practical vocational nursing generally requires from nine to eighteen months, but most schools average about one year of full-time study. The training usually is available through such public programs as adult education or vocational high schools and less often through hospitals, junior colleges, or other associate degree programs.

The 1996 survey by the National League for Nursing showed, nationwide, a total of 238,244 students enrolled in undergraduate baccalaureate programs, 103,213 in associate programs, and

12,789 in diploma programs. Of these, 9,227 were black, 10,529 were Latino, and 1,816 were Asian, revealing a 20 percent increase in minority student enrollment in 1995.

Enrollment of men in nursing school has tended to level off at 12 percent, with an increase since 2000. According to the survey, male students numbered 10,263 in baccalaureate programs, 12,144 in associate degree programs, and 1,382 in diploma programs.

Entrance requirements vary with the nature of the program, and most require the completion or the equivalent of a high school diploma. However, some programs require only completion of eighth grade, and others depend on age and other factors as criteria for admission acceptability. As schools of practical nursing redesign and alter their curricula, focusing on a more open-ended course of study, increased numbers of students with backgrounds in the health field apply. Individuals with experience as nursing assistants or in the military medical corps may be able to expedite the study period through advanced standing or challenge exams. Nontraditional programs and credit for knowledge are current educational trends, particularly for adult learners.

The typical course of study in a practical nursing program consists of a core course in science, one in the behavioral sciences, and a course in the basics of providing nursing care for each of five major disease categories—medicine, surgery, obstetrics, pediatrics, and psychiatry.

A typical course of study in a program for practical nursing might be:

First Semester	**Second Semester**
Normal Nutrition	Care of Mothers and
Elementary Nursing	Newborns
Procedures	Care of Children

Family Living, Growth, and Development	Care of Mental Patients
	Diet Therapy
Medical and Surgical Nursing	Drugs and their
Body Structure and Function	Administration

The emphasis in a practical nursing program is on the clinical or hospital experience. The student's time is directed toward providing patient care and the performance of technical skills. A typical student day might consist of the hours between 8:00 A.M. and 1:00 P.M. in a hospital giving direct patient care, followed by a class from 2:00 to 4:00 P.M. The cost of practical nursing programs varies from little tuition to $5,000 per year, in addition to room and board. Upon successful completion of a practical nursing program, the graduate receives a diploma or certificate of completion. The graduate is then permitted to take the licensing examination. If passed, the state board of nursing issues a license permitting the nurse to legally use the title of L.V.N. or L.P.N. Not all states require practical or vocational nurses to be licensed, but they all support the idea of mandatory licensure.

A license is good for the state in which the exam was taken and passed. It gives the nurse the legal right to practice as a licensed practical nurse in the state that issued the license. Since each state has slightly different minimum standards and requirements, the practical nurse with a license in one state must apply for licensure to practice in another state. This is usually a matter of checking records and does not require taking another examination.

Licensed practical nurses work in hospitals, extended-care facilities, nursing homes, clinics, or physicians' offices. It is advisable for the L.P.N. to become a member of the National Federation of Licensed Practical Nurses. It is through this national nursing organization that leaders in practical nursing hope to maintain their members' identity and support and protect the development of practical nursing.

Career mobility for the practical nurse is possible, but it is important to choose a nursing program very carefully because preparation for a different career is costly in both time and money.

Advancement for the practical nurse usually depends on additional education; nursing positions with added responsibility require registered nurse status. Some L.P.N. programs are now proposing specialty preparation at the L.P.N. level. Most schools preparing nurses at the R.N. level offer courses with more depth and scientific sophistication; however, some L.P.N.s might find repetition in an R.N. program of some material they have already studied, making it unadvisable for them to view their L.P.N. training as a basis for an R.N. program.

There are a few schools offering associate degrees in nursing whose programs are designed for the practical nurse. Such schools give full or almost full credit for practical nursing education and provide an additional year for the completion of an associate degree in nursing. Graduates of these programs are also eligible for the registered nurse examination.

Professional Registered Nurse Programs: The Baccalaureate Degree

Individuals who complete the course of study for a baccalaureate degree in nursing are eligible for the registered nurse licensure examination. Graduates of baccalaureate programs also are prepared to seek direct admission to master's degree programs. In addition, nurses with bachelor's degrees are prepared to plan and provide care to patients and their families and to assume beginning leadership positions as coordinators of the health care team. The baccalaureate graduate is able to perform in a variety of health care settings, including such areas as well-baby clinics, health promotion agencies, and hospitals.

Baccalaureate Education

The baccalaureate degree program in nursing follows an educational pattern similar to the traditional program for other bachelor's degrees. As a result, nursing students complete a combination of general liberal arts courses, along with specialized professional nursing classes and clinical laboratory experience.

Nurses with professional education are capable of evaluating incoming information and judging its relevance to the problems at hand. In *Nursing Outlook*, Fay Carol Reed states: "Teachers in baccalaureate programs stress those learning experiences, theoretical and practical, which assist students to develop skills in recognizing and solving problems, applying general principles to particular situations, and establishing a basis for making sound judgments. This emphasis deters students from developing the idea that their education has been a process of acquiring a set of facts and solutions which may be applied to situations encountered later. Thus the nurse who is a graduate of a baccalaureate degree program should distinguish herself from graduates of other types of educational programs in nursing by her ability to apply intelligence and knowledge freely to those problems which she experiences in her practice."

She also explains, "Graduates of baccalaureate programs are distinguished by the quality of mind which seeks to test solutions to problems and to cope with unfamiliar situations. And these graduates differ in the kind, quality, and quantity of knowledge they are able to bring to bear on complex problems." Essentially, the role of the baccalaureate degree nurse is planning and providing care, particularly in situations that are out of the ordinary, and supervising the care provided by subordinate health team members.

The baccalaureate program is best suited to those individuals whose interests are in a senior college or a university-based education. This type of program leads to a B.S. in nursing or to eligibility for licensure as an R.N. Approximately four academic years are needed to complete the program.

Baccalaureate degree programs in nursing are offered through many colleges and universities. Similar to the associate degree programs, there is an increasing trend toward baccalaureate preparation. As of 1992 there were 1,484 baccalaureate degree nursing programs, up from 483 in 1987. As of 1996 the total number of nursing school graduates in the United States were as follows: 32,413 baccalaureate degrees, 56,641 associate degrees, and 5,703 diploma graduates. (In 1996 there were 94,757 R.N.s and 44,234 L.P.N./L.V.N.s.) Compare these totals to the total number of nursing school graduates in 1980: 24,994 baccalaureate degrees, 36,034 associate degrees, and 14,495 diploma graduates. (In 1980 there were 75,523 R.N.s and 41,892 L.P.N./L.V.N.s.)

Also similar to the associate degree nursing programs is the advantage that all students seeking admittance are evaluated according to the same intellectual and academic standards as students in other fields. Additionally, the quality of both types of nursing education is high because the nursing faculty must meet the same educational and experience standards as other college teachers.

Tuition and living expenses for nursing students are very similar to those of other students on campus. There is, again, a difference between tuition charges for residents within a local state university system and a private college or university.

Admission requirements vary, depending on the overall college or university standards. The variations are as wide as open admissions in certain colleges to high minimum SAT scores for an Ivy League school. In addition, the prospective student will be expected to meet the entrance standards set up by the nursing program. Just as in the associate degree program, it is important for prospective applicants to obtain school catalogs or bulletins early, preferably during high school, to get some idea of the requirements for admission.

Course of Study

The course of study in the baccalaureate degree program consists of such liberal arts courses as English and philosophy; science courses in biology, chemistry, and psychology; and courses in the theory and practice of nursing. Students also learn nursing practice in a variety of clinical laboratory settings including clinics, community agencies, and health-related facilities.

The importance of preparing at the baccalaureate level in nursing has received continuous emphasis among nursing leaders, educators, and administrators. As a result, baccalaureate nursing programs provide a wide range of flexibility and options for high school graduates. Nursing programs awarding bachelor's degrees organize their curricula in two ways. The *upper-division program* concentrates on nursing theory and practice courses in the junior and senior years, while most of the liberal arts and science courses are completed during the freshman and sophomore years. This type of program allows students to attend a junior college or another university for the freshman and sophomore years, then transfer to the nursing program for the final two years. The other type of program is called a *generic* or *integrated program*. The generic program integrates nursing courses with the liberal arts and sciences, beginning in either the freshman year or first semester of the sophomore year. Either program is appropriate for high school graduates.

College graduates or students with college experience who wish to major in nursing also have several options available to them. For example, a number of programs admit college graduates, regardless of their majors, and offer a four-semester nursing program that awards a master's degree in nursing. Equally appropriate, particularly for students who have completed two years of college, are the upper-division programs, in which the nursing major is concentrated into two years. For example, a few programs require two years of college prior to admission to the four-semester nursing program. It is important, however, to determine as early as possible the college courses required for entrance into either type of nursing program. Most often they include courses such as literature or art, biology, general chemistry (two semesters), microbiology, anthropology, general psychology, human anatomy and physiology (two semesters), English, human development, and physics. The final choice would be to pursue a generic program on a part-time basis, taking only the nursing courses required. This can be very costly and time-consuming, as many universities and colleges charge tuition by the credit hour up to twelve hours; at that point, a student is considered full-time and is charged a fixed rate.

Registered nurses who have earned associate degrees or have graduated from hospital programs may also choose from several R.N. programs through which they may earn a baccalaureate degree in nursing. For example, one college in Pennsylvania admits registered nurses and awards a baccalaureate degree following completion of its two-year program in nursing. It requires as a prerequisite the equivalent of an associate degree, either through actual course work or challenge exams. Practicing nurses may also select a nursing program that offers challenge exams in the nursing content course or other special arrangements for evaluating the nurse's knowledge of baccalaureate-level nursing theory and practice.

A word of caution is in order at this point, particularly to registered nurses seeking advanced college degrees. Many health care agencies and institutions require their nurses to obtain a bachelor's degree; however, beware of the programs that offer a B.S. to nurses in health education, health administration, and occupational health. For nurses, these degrees are not the equivalent of a B.S. in nursing and are not acceptable as appropriate preparation for advanced nursing education such as a master's in nursing or some of the nurse practitioner programs. If you have any doubt about the degree, the program, or its appropriateness for nursing preparation, contact either your state nurses' association or the National League for Nursing.

Nursing programs that award baccalaureate degrees organize their curricula in one of two ways. In the upper-division program, where the nursing courses are concentrated entirely in the junior and senior years, the program of study might be constructed as follows:

Freshman Year

First Semester	Second Semester
Biology—Introduction	Anatomy
Chemistry I	Chemistry II
English I	English II
Psychology I	Psychology II
Precalculus Math	Sociology

Sophomore Year

First Semester	Second Semester
Cultural Anthropology	Microbiology
Organic Chemistry	Physiology
Introduction to Philosophy	Art Elective
Physics	Sociology
Elective	Elective

Junior Year

First Semester	Second Semester
Fundamentals of Nursing	Growth and Development
Nursing Trends	Nursing Adults II
Nursing Adults I	Epidemiology
Nutrition	Parent-Child Nursing I

Senior Year

First Semester	Second Semester
Psychiatric Nursing	Health Care in the
Parent-Child Nursing II	Social System
Introduction to Nursing	Advanced Nursing Elective
Research	Nursing in the Community

The program of study for the baccalaureate student is quite demanding both in time and intensity. The nursing courses and many of the sciences include a laboratory component. As a result, a typical student four-day week may include an 8:00 A.M. to 1:00 P.M. clinical nursing laboratory in a nursing home, a 4:00 to 6:00 P.M. sociology class, and a 6:00 to 8:00 P.M. nursing theory class, depending on the course and the student's schedule. On the other hand, a student may elect to schedule classes lightly each day but spread them out over five days.

The student who completes a baccalaureate degree in nursing is eligible to take the state board examination, which licenses registered nurses. As an R.N. the nurse is then legally qualified to practice in the state where the licensing examination was passed.

Graduate Education

Many nurses today are pursuing higher-education degrees as the means by which they can advance in their field. Increases in technology and research have opened the doors to jobs that require even more sophistication and skill than ever before.

Master's Education

Nurses who wish to pursue graduate-level study in a master's program have more than sixty programs to select from; however, the programs vary according to the philosophy and nature of the school and its faculty. Some programs offer a master's degree in nursing education or administration, while others may focus on various nursing clinical specialties, such as geriatrics, medical-surgical, or community health.

At present, nursing is in need of many more nurses who are prepared at the master's level. Nursing currently requires individuals who are able to advance the quality of nursing care as clinicians, educators, and administrators. Master's-level nursing programs prepare such nurses.

As nursing becomes more sophisticated theoretically and educationally, such jobs as nursing administrator, nurse educator or in-service instructor, clinical specialist, or nurse consultant, will require a minimum of a master's degree in nursing. Most programs are one-and-a-half to two years in length or require from forty to sixty college credits following the completion of a baccalaureate degree in nursing.

The best source for the names, addresses, types of programs, and other important details is a pamphlet published by the National League for Nursing entitled "Master's List for Schools in the Country." Find the NLN on the Internet or write it at 305 Hudson Street, New York, New York 10014, attention "Career Advancement."

Doctoral Education

Currently there are approximately eight to ten thousand nurses in the United States who have earned doctorates. This is a remarkable figure considering that it represents only 0.3 percent of all registered nurses. It is important for a profession to have some of its members prepared at the doctoral level, because such individuals are responsible for the growth and leadership of the profession. Nurses with doctorates should be educated to be nursing scholars and researchers and should assume a leadership role by formulating and testing nursing theory and providing direction to the profession of nursing. At present there are fifty-seven programs for nurses in the United States that award a doctorate in nursing.

There is debate among nursing leaders about the desirability of nurses earning doctorates in disciplines other than nursing, such as anthropology, sociology, or biology. Some believe that the doctorate in nursing ensures educational socialization and identification with nursing. Others believe that nursing theory draws from many disciplines, and, therefore, nurses with doctorates from other disciplines will be able to add another dimension to nursing knowledge. However, it does seem that the trend, based on the current number of programs, is toward doctoral preparation for nurses in the nursing discipline.

Nurses with doctorates usually assume such positions as deans of university- and college-based schools of nursing, as directors of nursing service in the larger medical centers, as nurse researchers, and as faculty members in baccalaureate, master's, and doctoral programs in nursing. Generally they are expected to design and implement research in their positions as that is a primary purpose of doctoral education.

Nontraditional Approaches

There are a number of nontraditional educational programs in nursing, particularly within the college or university setting, that offer diplomas or degrees. Most of these programs award credit (or advanced placement) according to prior knowledge and competencies. One particularly interesting program is the Regents External Degree Program offered through the University of the State of New York. This program offers an associate and a bachelor's degree in nursing and essentially is not responsible for teaching the students. The students are awarded an A.A., A.A.S., or B.S. when they have demonstrated that they possess the prescribed knowledge and ability for such a degree. In the liberal arts, students may accumulate the necessary credits by completing accredited military or accredited college courses or by passing such college-level proficiency examinations as the College Entrance Examination Board's College-Level Examination.

In this particular nontraditional program, knowledge of nursing theory and demonstration of nursing skills are tested by a number of unwritten examinations. For the associate degree, there is one test on clinical performance given in a hospital setting where the student is expected to provide direct care to patients. For the baccalaureate degree, there is an additional clinical performance exam related to leadership skills.

In planning your nursing education, make certain that the program you select accurately reflects your long-range career goals. To be sure that you are on the right path, you should discuss your educational and occupational goals with nurse educators in your community, with your high school guidance counselors, and with your family.

Selecting a School

Selecting an appropriate nursing school and program can be difficult, but the process will be much less complex if you are absolutely certain that you want to study nursing as a career. If you are unsure about your ability or desire to become a nurse, you should try out the nursing field as a nurse's aide in a hospital or other health care facility. Such positions usually are not very difficult to find, particularly during the summer or for the evening and night shifts. If you can't find a salaried position, offer your services as a volunteer. The experience you will gain from such work will be extremely valuable to you later in your nursing career.

If after the test period nursing is still appealing to you, begin investigating schools early. Each has different requirements and some have waiting lists, making it essential for you to evaluate school catalogs carefully and complete the application process accurately and well in advance of deadlines. Some of your general questions regarding nursing schools and programs may have been answered earlier in this chapter. However, for specific information you should write to the National League for Nursing (NLN) or go to its website at nln.org to find lists of accredited educational programs in each of the categories discussed. Each bulletin gives a description of the graduates, how to select schools, and specific information about each school including admission criteria, cost, length of study, and addresses. Write to:

National League for Nursing
305 Hudson Street
New York, New York 10014

When you receive the pamphlets or Internet information, review the material briefly and write for catalogs of the schools that interest you most or go to their Internet websites. The school catalogs will list criteria for admission, individual curricula, and other pertinent information.

Accreditation

As you examine the bulletins, note whether the programs have been accredited and by whom. Accreditation means that the school has applied for and been granted approval for its programs by the state in which it is located, by the National League for Nursing, or by the American Association of Colleges of Nursing. Each state must award schools of nursing permission to operate legally through its board of nurse examiners.

The National League for Nursing offers voluntary accreditation based on national standards. The league employs criteria that are designed to accredit quality programs and maintain high standards. It applies its standards to programs preparing practical and registered nurses in associate, hospital, baccalaureate, and master's degree programs. The evaluation measures, which were designed by nursing experts, examine the program's curriculum, how it is implemented, and the preparation of the faculty. Although accreditation by the National League for Nursing is not required, a majority of nursing programs have sought its approval and have received accreditation. Currently, many programs awarding master's and/or doctorate degrees in nursing require for admission graduation from an NLN-approved undergraduate program. In addition, a number of state and federal financial aid programs offer funds only to NLN-accredited schools.

The other accrediting agency is the American Association of Colleges of Nursing (AACN). This organization accredits only baccalaureate and master's degree programs, whereas the NLN accredits associate, baccalaureate, and master's degree programs as well as practical nursing and diploma programs.

Application

As soon as you have selected one or more schools that seem to meet your individual needs and goals, begin the application process as soon as possible. For many nursing programs it is best to apply during your junior year in high school. Schools will probably require recommendations from teachers, personal reference letters, and a copy of your high school transcript, and you should submit these promptly.

You may find it helpful to visit the schools you have selected to get more information about the student population and campus and community facilities. During your visit, you might also have an opportunity to talk with a few students who are already enrolled in the nursing program.

Financial Assistance

The cost of post–high school education is constantly increasing, and nursing programs are no exception to this trend. Frequently, prospective nurses select an educational program solely on the basis of their financial resources. There is certainly a wide difference in cost between a two-year associate degree program at a public college and four years at a senior college. However, the purposes of the programs differ, and they prepare nurses for essentially two different careers.

Students who anticipate a need for financial assistance have available to them a number of resources. Most nursing programs award a number of scholarships and grants each year. They are usually based on financial need, scholastic and intellectual ability, and potential in the field of nursing. You can get more information about these by writing to the school you have selected.

Such organizations as the Elks, American Legion, and the American Association of University Women also offer scholarships and/or loans, as do many churches and other religious organizations. Also, most states award incentive scholarships and/or loans. Your state department of education or high school guidance counselor can provide you with lists of these as well as other lists of educational funds available to residents. The federal government also offers a variety of grants and scholarships. Information concerning these may be obtained by writing to the addresses below; each offers a separate type of loan or scholarship arrangement:

Office of Guaranteed Student Loans
U.S. Office of Education
Washington, D.C. 20202

Basic Grants
P.O. Box 84
Washington, D.C. 20044

Division of Nursing
Bureau of Health Manpower
Health Resources Administration
9000 Rockville Plaza
Bethesda, Maryland 20014

Chief Program Coordination Branch
Division of Disadvantage Assistance
Bureau of Health Professions
Parklawn Building, Room 8A-08
5600 Fishers Lane
Rockville, Maryland 20857

In addition, there are special funds available for minority group members and for veterans and their dependents. There is also a special program for students sponsored by both the army and navy corps, whereby students in a B.S. program in nursing may apply for appointment in the Army Student Nurse Program or the Navy Nurse Corps Program. Students accepted receive generous financial assistance toward tuition, room and board, and books. In return, students are expected to serve a specified time on active duty. For further information contact the local army or navy recruitment office.

Grants funded by institutionally and federally sponsored programs are awarded to students based on academic excellence and/or financial need and other personal circumstances.

Hospitals will finance nursing education, with a stipulation that before granting available funds, the student will agree to work for that hospital for a specific amount of time after graduation.

There are also a variety of pamphlets available about loans and scholarships. Probably the best and most comprehensive are:

A Guide to Student Assistance (Stock #052-071-00065-8)
U.S. Government Printing Office
Superintendent of Documents
P.O. Box 371954
Pittsburgh, Pennsylvania 15250-7954

Scholarships and Loans for Beginning Education in Nursing
    (Publication #41-410)
National League for Nursing
305 Hudson Street
New York, New York 10014
nln.org

The latter is probably the most comprehensive compilation of financial sources and resources for students enrolled in beginning nurse education programs.

4

STARTING YOUR CAREER

NURSING STUDENTS USUALLY begin to select areas of professional interest while still in school. By graduation most have identified clinical settings in which they would like to work. Some graduates may decide to continue their education, either working toward an advanced degree or furthering their knowledge and skills in a specialty area within a practitioner program. However, most nurse educators and administrators are opposed to this; they believe that graduates need employment experience to translate nursing education into practice.

Prior to graduation it is advisable for nursing students to speak with their career or guidance counselors about postgraduation plans. The counselor may be able to offer good advice and suggest some potential employers. Additionally, since most potential employers send requests for recommendations on applicants directly to school counselors, it is essential for the counselors to be well acquainted with students who are seeking employment.

The Importance of Self-Assessment

Self-assessment most naturally is a continuous process and ideally should be the basis for choosing nursing as a career. Often dissatisfaction with nursing is due to a poor match between the individual's personality and the nature, rewards, and problems that are a part of nursing.

Before selecting a job, it is important to review who you are—to identify the characteristics or traits that fit together to form your personality. The nurse who has self-awareness will more likely select a job that is compatible with what he or she values in a work situation. In many ways early self-assessment is the first step in career planning. Defining who you are is necessary before you can decide where you want to go.

According to a recent article in the *American Journal of Nursing*, one approach to self-assessment is to evaluate your preferences and abilities in the following areas: manual skills, temperament, interpersonal skills, stamina, role preferences, and cognitive skills. How you rate yourself in each area will offer guidance in identifying positions and situations that will be rewarding.

Manual Skills

Manual skills are required to some degree for all entry-level staff nurses. At the end of nursing school, most graduates have acquired a beginning skill with nursing procedures. Your answers to the following questions will help guide you when you are ready to select a specialty.

- Do I prefer working with new equipment and the latest in mechanical technology?

- Do I become tense when I have unexpected and/or complex treatments to perform?
- Is there an age group that I feel particularly comfortable or uncomfortable with when administering treatments?

The nurse who indicates that he or she is most comfortable in situations where there is an emphasis on drama and technical skills would prefer an intensive care unit or operating room to a physician's office.

Temperament

Temperament refers to the pace an individual prefers and includes the amount and frequency of stress he or she can tolerate. Certain situations such as the emergency room are good for the nurse who enjoys activity, change, and unpredictable situations. On the other hand, an outpatient clinic may be an ideal place for the nurse who is well suited to a slower, more regular pace. Answering the following questions may be helpful.

- Do I become easily bored by routine?
- Do I feel the most invigorated when I have two or three projects going at the same time?
- Do I enjoy solving frustrating problems that others cannot?

There is nothing unhappier than a slow-paced worker in a fast-paced system or an activity-oriented worker in a quiet system.

Interpersonal Skills

Interpersonal skills are a part of all nursing. During any exchange between people it is impossible not to communicate. Since nursing requires exchange, interpersonal skills are needed. However, different nursing settings require varying degrees of interaction. For example, the basis for psychiatric nursing is communication with the patient. On the other hand, the nurse in an intensive care unit is more involved with observing monitors and recording data than with interacting with the patient. Also, the nature of the interaction between nurse and patient is different. The psychiatric nurse focuses on the patient's emotional status and patterns of communication. The intensive care unit nurse concentrates more on the patient's physical status and the emotional reactions to the physical problems. The following questions may help you assess your interpersonal preferences.

- Do I enjoy conversing with others, or am I more comfortable as an observer?
- When others are upset, do I feel comfortable giving them support?
- Am I a good listener?

Stamina

Stamina is physical energy, which can reach high and low points over the course of the day. Determining under what conditions you feel most energetic is important. Conditions such as warm versus cold and seasonal changes—sunny, cloudy, or misty—are a few examples. Here are some questions that may help you measure your level of stamina.

- Do I tire easily and/or under what conditions do I tire?
- What situations make me feel more energetic?
- Am I physically able to perform various nursing tasks?

Role Position Preference

Role position preference will help you determine the kind of position in which you would function the best. Role includes ideas such as assuming amounts of responsibility, supervising others or being supervised, working alone or in groups, and working in a leadership position or in a clinical practice situation. The following questions will help you determine the role situation you would find most rewarding.

- Do I prefer to have others guide my work?
- Do I enjoy assuming responsibility for others?
- Do I prefer working alone or with groups?

Cognitive Skills

Cognitive skills are part of intelligence, but more so they involve the ability to think through, problem solve, and analyze situations based on previous experience. People with strong cognitive skills prefer new and novel situations, have the desire to constantly be learning, and rely on memory. Answers to questions such as the following will help you determine your level of cognitive skills.

- Do I prefer to explore new situations more by myself, or do I prefer the support of others?
- Do I enjoy learning as a part of my life, or is it a struggle?
- Am I more stimulated by learning a few things well, or is it better for me to learn many things rapidly?

When the time comes to select a job, each of these variables will influence your final decision. So will your personal lifestyle. If you are married, you may select a job primarily because of its regular hours and free weekends, so that you can be home at the same time as your spouse and children. Or you may select a part-time job for only a few hours each day so you can give maximum time to your family. On the other hand, if you are a young, single nurse, you may give high priority to a geographical location where employment or social opportunities are great or where top salaries are paid. Still other nurses with graduate degrees may select university or research settings that encourage and enhance professional development and study. In such cases, salary and geographic location may be only secondary considerations during the job search and selection process.

Be sure that you take stock of and assign your own priorities to factors such as job location, salary, hours, professional environment, opportunity for advancement, and family needs or obligations. You might also want to take into consideration other factors, such as big versus small clinics and attitudes of coworkers, when you evaluate job offers. Once you have determined which factors are of the greatest importance to you, the job selection process will be much easier.

Potential Employment Sources

Nursing students preparing for graduation should begin considering and applying for jobs four to six months prior to graduation. Some nursing experts advise initiating this earlier in the educational process, believing that this will stimulate the student to identify and evaluate specific areas of interest. However, basic nursing education in any of the programs is truly preparation at the generalist level. This means that the education introduces in a limited way almost all facets of nursing. Often students may not get clinical experience in the area that they may eventually select for specialization until their final semester.

Many students find that applying for a position in the clinical, hospital, or community setting where their nursing practice as a student was done increases the probability of securing a job. To ensure immediate licensure, it is especially important for graduating nurses to determine where they intend to practice; there is, however, reciprocity of licensure between many states. To qualify for licensure examination by the state board of nursing, applicants must submit certain forms in advance. Information regarding the fees, eligibility, and the schedule of where and when the exam will be given may be obtained by writing to the state board of nursing for the particular state it is being taken in. State boards and their addresses are included in Appendix B.

A nurse who is licensed in one state and wishes to be licensed in another should also write to the state board of nursing in the state where he or she wishes to be licensed. The board will mail the forms and requirements for reciprocity (licensure in one state based on the examination scores from another). The licensure process for the new state usually takes from three to six months. However, most states and health care agencies make provisions for working under a temporary permit. Such provisions are also made for the new graduate who has not yet taken and/or received scores from the licensure examination. Temporary permits in both instances are usually valid for approximately six months.

In searching for a job, there are a number of resources that traditionally prove to be valuable. In *Dimensions of Professional Nursing*, Lucie Kelly lists the following five as the most productive:

1. personal contacts and inquiries
2. counseling and placement services

3. magazine and newspaper advertisements
4. approved nurses' registries
5. commercial placement agencies

Personal Contacts and Inquiries

Personal contacts and inquiries are usually very effective. They include recommendations from friends, colleagues, or academic counselors about agencies or settings in the student's field of interest that might be hiring or accepting inquiries.

Inquiries can be very productive job sources. Begin by obtaining a list of names and short descriptions of the services offered by all of the health care and/or social institutions in the desired geographic area(s). Then select those agencies that seem most appropriate and promising, and forward to each a letter of introduction and a personal résumé. It is a good idea to place a follow-up phone call to the personnel office to be sure the letter was received and to establish contact with the agency. This method often produces very satisfactory and sometimes surprisingly successful results. It is not uncommon for an institution or agency that has no openings to respond by advising you of neighboring facilities that might. It may even provide addresses.

Counseling and Placement Services

Junior colleges and universities usually maintain free counseling and placement services. When they register, graduates or near-graduates are placed on a list to receive regular bulletins regarding job opportunities in their fields of specialization and interest, such as nursing or medical-surgical nursing education. In addition, the service collects information about the applicant's educational and professional experience. The agency then places this on file and mails copies at the request of the individual to agencies or institutions that have job openings. Some state nurses associations also provide a job advisory service and share with applicants names and/or locations where employment potential is good. The names and addresses for each state nurses association are included in Appendix A.

Magazine and Newspaper Advertisements

Professional nursing journals and related publications, and most newspapers, include a section of advertisements regarding available positions. These can be good sources of information because they give very specific details about available positions. The "Positions Available" section of national journals will also provide an idea of the nature of positions open in various areas of the country. For example, in the northeastern United States there may be few openings for staff nurses but many for administrative nurses. This may be an indication that new positions have opened up at higher levels and that there is plenty of room for advancement, or it may mean that this area of the country has an oversupply of staff-level nurses.

Registries and Agencies

In each state, professional registries maintain lists of licensed nurses who meet eligibility requirements and refer patients needing care to these practitioners. Each state nursing association approves professional registries according to stringent criteria to ensure quality nursing care in the community. Requests for nursing services are filled by the registry after the nature and complexity of the individual case and the qualifications and backgrounds of the nurses registered have been considered.

Commercial registries must be licensed by the state to operate. However, very few additional regulatory mechanisms guarantee quality service to either the nurse or the patient/client. Some commercial registries, however, are quite careful about informing the nurse and patient/client about their fees and selecting the appropriate nurse for the case. Most can be found in the yellow pages of the phone directory, or they may advertise in the local newspaper. Prior to accepting a case or a position from this source, it is important to be well informed about the policies, practices, and procedures of the commercial registry.

Some hospitals use a registry or agency to supplement their permanent staff. Generally the daily rate paid by the registry is considerably higher (20 percent to 30 percent) than that paid the staff nurse. However, the advantages and disadvantages are based on the difference between an employee of an institution and the self-employed. The benefits that are a part of the staff nurse's salary usually include a forty-hour workweek, continuing education program, paid vacation, paid sick time, insurance, retirement benefits, tuition reimbursement, career advancement, shift options, job and financial security, and a place in staff/administration meetings, according to the *National Nursing News.*

The registry nurse often has different personal and career goals and has no loyalty to the hospital. Registry nurses are free to select their time and the unit and/or type of patient they wish to care for. They are truly free agents. The registry nurse has the right to say no to various nursing issues within the institution. This may appeal to some but represents a source of frustration for others.

A final word to those graduate nurses with an adventurous spirit. Graduate nurses have been known to pack their bags and travel around the country seeking employment. Because nurses are in demand, most find jobs rather easily during their travels. One nurse traveled from the east to the west, stopping at various points, volunteering nursing services at an Indian reservation, and collecting per diem (day-to-day) wages at a variety of hospitals in places like Kansas City, Cleveland, and Denver. She finally settled (temporarily) in San Francisco, where she found a job quite soon after her arrival by talking directly with nursing personnel directors. However, not many individuals are able to withstand the discomfort and insecurity of constant travel just for the sake of adventure; make sure before you strike out on such an odyssey that you have the stamina to keep going.

The Internet

With today's technology, the early phases of searching for a job can be done using the Internet. Once logged on, enter the terms "nursing employment" or "jobs for nurses" as well as the name of the city in which you would like to work. You can then pick and choose among the "hits" you would like to explore.

Preparing a Résumé

Prospective employers usually require a written summary of an applicant's biographical data, including information about education and job experience. This summary is called a *résumé* (sometimes referred to as a *curriculum vitae*). It is important that the résumé be written and organized in a professional manner because it may serve as the applicant's introduction to an employer. A neatly typed, logically organized résumé gives a good first impression; one that is poorly written and typed with mistakes, smudges, and erasures will not enhance an applicant's image.

The purpose of the résumé is to acquaint the prospective employer with the candidate in a condensed form. The format is fairly standard but varies in content according to the applicant's experience and education.

A typical résumé begins with such identifying data as name, address, phone number, and date of birth. Do not include personal facts, such as marital and citizenship status, sex, children, spouse's occupation, and height and weight. Such information can bias a prospective employer, and it is illegal for an employer to ask for such information unless it directly relates to the job. If you have a specific job in mind, you may wish to include a one-sentence statement of your objective.

The section concerning educational preparation usually follows next and should contain information such as the name and address of all schools attended as well as the degree earned, the major area of study, and all dates of attendance. This section should begin with the school from which the nursing diploma was granted and then continue to list in reverse chronological order each school attended. Since the employment experience section of newly graduated nurses often is limited, it is best to highlight educational preparation. It would be appropriate to include brief details about course titles and content and the nature of the clinical experience. Be particularly certain to mention those courses that relate directly to areas of employment interest.

The last section is employment or professional experience. List all job or job-related responsibilities, beginning with the most recent position. It is helpful to include details such as the name and address of each institution or agency, dates of employment, exact job titles, and a brief synopsis of the responsibilities and description of the position.

A list of memberships in professional and professionally related organizations should follow. Be sure to write out the complete title of the organization, as abbreviations or acronyms may be confusing or misunderstood. (ANA in nursing circles does stand for American Nurses Association, but it also represents the letters for the American Numismatic Association—a group of coin collectors!) It is also important to include the status of the membership if this is relevant—for example, student, full clinical member, or professional member.

Because nurses must be licensed to practice, a separate section of the résumé should list states where licensure or temporary certification is held, followed by the state license number.

Involvement in community organizations often reflects a community sense of responsibility. These should be listed with dates and, if applicable, executive offices held. It would be appropriate to include activities such as Girl Scout troop leader, Little League coach, or volunteer for the United Farm Workers' Association.

Depending on individual interests and qualifications, there may be additional headings such as consultations, publications, professionally related activities, major papers presented, awards received, and/or workshops presented. Since the résumé is a summary of an individual's qualifications, preparation, and competencies, it is important to include all activities that might help to reflect such characteristics.

Some registered nurses prefer to use the résumé service provided by the American Nurses Association's Professional Credentials and Personnel Service. This service is offered to members of the American Nurses Association for a small fee, and, on request, it will send copies of the participant's records and recommendations from instructors and colleagues to prospective employers or give them to whomever the participating nurse requests. This is a valuable service because it saves faculty, employers, and personal references

Melinda Weston Strause
84 East Circle Avenue
Neston, Massachusetts 02134
(502) 555-6910

Objective:
Staff nurse responsible for providing nursing care to groups of patients in a neurological unit—medical or surgical.

Education:
Nestleton College, New York, New York
B.S. in Nursing, May 2002

Studied advanced nursing, a course that required 150 hours of clinical experience divided among neurosurgical, medical neurology, and neurological intensive care units. Acquired 150 hours of clinical experience in Nursing Science III by caring for patients in complex situations including diabetic crises, brain tumors, and cardiac monitor units.

Experience:
July 2002–present: Leston General Hospital, Retlin, New York, staff nurse. As an L.P.N., provide direct total care to approximately eight to ten patients on a general postsurgical unit.

1999–2002: Mercy Hope Hospital, Bixby, Pennsylvania, candy striper volunteer. Provided services such as reading to visually impaired adults and children in an orthopedic unit. Received first "Teenage Volunteer" award for two hundred hours of service.

Certification:
Licensed as registered professional nurse:
New York, license number 12345678.

Awards and Honors:
Outstanding Senior, Nestleton College, 2002
Dean's List, Nestleton College, 2000–2001
Student Government Association
President, Future Nurses Club

from repeatedly writing letters for each former nursing student or employee. Each time the résumé requires updating, letters of recommendation from recent jobs are written by the employer and become part of a permanent file, which is then available on request.

The sample résumé shown is an example of one that a recent nurse graduate might compile.

The Interview

Few places will hire an employee without a face-to-face interview. This meeting is necessary for both sides to evaluate each other and can be very beneficial. Viewing the interview as an opportunity, the prospective employee should be prepared with both questions and answers. The applicant who follows certain guidelines has a greater chance for selecting and landing a job that is both appropriate and satisfying.

A specific time for the interview should be set in advance, giving consideration to such matters as weather, travel time, directions, and scheduling. Applicants who arrive late for interviews often give a first impression of tardiness; applicants who arrive for interviews a little early have time to relax and collect their thoughts, making the interview atmosphere calm and unhurried. It is best to control and minimize anything that might contribute to any further tension than a normal interview produces. The interview length varies, but ordinarily it runs from twenty to forty minutes for staff nursing positions to three hours or more for prospective university nursing faculty.

Besides educational and experiential credentials, most prospective employers consider two other factors that affect their decisions about hiring. The first is attire, and the second is attitude.

The new graduate nurse who arrives looking neat and speaking with enthusiasm has a better chance for a position than one who looks disorganized and bored. On the other hand, it is important to attend a job interview dressed comfortably and consistently with good taste.

Another suggestion for approaching an interview is to be prepared to answer questions that logically arise; additionally applicants should point out their assets as well as their shortcomings, without dwelling on either. For instance, newly graduated nurses sometimes are concerned about their comparative lack of experience. Although it is appropriate to acknowledge this, the applicant should also emphasize that the desire to learn, combined with in-service and continuing education and the opportunity to practice, often compensates for any lack in experience. Regarding this situation, Rachel Rotkovich, a leading nurse administrator, said: "I don't expect her to be expert in the technical skills nurses use in the care of patients. If a nurse understands the principles and theory which underlie the various nursing interventions, then our in-service clinicians on all three shifts will have a good foundation on which to build. The result is an efficient and competent professional nurse practitioner."

Another question often raised is the applicant's philosophy of nursing or nursing care. This is important, because many nurses have not given any thought to a conscious foundation on which to base nursing care. Often this lack of a philosophy is very apparent, particularly if the nurse's approach to patients seems to be disorganized and lacking in purpose. Other questions might include projected long-term career plans, thoughts about continuing education, attitudes about current nursing issues such as proposed legislation for nurses, or ideas about particular types of nursing care—for example, how to treat a bedsore or an ulcer.

Applicants should also be prepared to ask questions of prospective employers. It is important to become familiar with the clinical area or unit in which the position is available as well as the nature and description of the care provided in the unit. Sometimes the initial description may be misleading, and it is wise to ask for a job description for the position in question. Similarly, it is important to question the employer about time scheduling: frequency of weekends off, frequency of evening and night shifts, and procedures for requesting days and time off.

Fringe benefits and salary vary according to the agency. Nurses traditionally have difficulties in securing adequate economic returns for their services. Fortunately this problem has diminished greatly, and most employers offer reasonable salary scales. However, the question of salary should be explored by considering the salary differential for evening and night hours and the criteria for and frequency of salary increases. Fringe benefits represent a financial outlay by the employer that is not reflected in the actual salary. These benefits may include paid vacations, tuition reimbursement or exemption, reimbursement for continuing education, a hospitalization and retirement plan, and reimbursed travel expenses for professional meetings.

If feasible during the interview, it is also revealing to take a tour of the facilities. During the tour, observe the total atmosphere—how staff members deal with each other and with patients. In addition, a walk around the facilities and neighborhood will provide information about the work environment—safety, access to shopping, and cultural resources.

An excellent additional resource is a paperback published annually by the American Journal of Nursing Company, entitled *The AJN Guide: A Review of Nursing Career Opportunities*. Copies are available to students on request by writing to the *AJN Guide*, American Journal of Nursing Company, G.P.O. Box 2913, New York, New York 10017. An excellent website that provides information about answering interview questions and offers a simulated interview can be found at job-interview.net. Further searching will reveal a number of other sites that offer excellent tips on how to handle a job interview.

5

Types and Places of Employment

The U.S. Department of Labor reports that in 2000 there were about 2.2 million registered nurses employed in the United States. These nurses provide nursing or nursing-related services in a wide variety of settings. Essentially, nursing care is needed wherever there are people; however, there are particular situations in which nurses are especially needed. These include positions in nursing service, nursing administration, nursing education, and nursing research. According to area of employment, most worked in an institutional setting, primarily hospitals. Almost 66.5 percent of all registered nurses were working in hospitals in 2000. Nursing homes employed 8 percent. In noninstitutional settings, 6 percent worked in a physician's or dentist's office, 7 percent in community or public health, 3 percent in educational services, 2 percent in personnel supply services, 3 percent in health and allied services not elsewhere classified, 3 percent in outpatient care facilities, and 1.5 percent in other areas.

Another perspective on employment is that about three out of five jobs were in hospitals—inpatient and outpatient departments. Others were mostly in offices and clinics of physicians and other health practitioners, home health care agencies, nursing homes, temporary help agencies, and schools and government agencies. The remainder worked for residential care facilities, social service agencies, religious organizations, research facilities, management and public relations firms, insurance agencies, and private households. About one out of four R.N.s worked part-time.

Nursing Service

Nursing service is probably the most well known and common employment area for nurses. More than half of all employed registered and licensed practical nurses are employed by hospitals, and almost three-quarters of all employed nurses provide direct nursing services to patients in settings such as public health agencies, nursing homes, hospitals, industrial settings, federal and government agencies, insurance companies, and various areas of business.

Staff Nurses

The position of staff nurse is probably the most common title given to the nurse who plans, administers, and evaluates the care given to a selected group of patients. In some health care settings, nurses may be categorized according to ability and qualifications, using titles such as senior or junior nurse or graduate designations of I, II, and III. In such instances, the job description and salaries vary according to the level of responsibility.

The staff nurse functions as a contributing member of the health team. The variations in the job description are usually the result of the health care setting. The staff nurse in a hospital setting typically has the opportunity for a wide variety of experiences. With the continued advancement of technology, many hospitals may now offer treatment on specialty units such as artificial kidney machine units or transplant units, and in various types of special intensive care areas such as cardiac or neurological.

The new staff nurse should anticipate an initial orientation period during which the policy and procedures of the hospital and the philosophy and nature of nursing care provided are taught. In addition, advice is given about the routine of each of the two or three nursing shifts that most hospitals employ.

In the 1996 sample survey of nursing employees, the salaries for hospital and staff nurses are varied according to educational preparation. Baccalaureate-prepared hospital nurses reported an average yearly salary of $41,053. Associate-prepared hospital nurses reported an average yearly salary of $37,936. R.N.s employed in nursing education had an average income of $44,197, followed by those working in hospitals whose average income reached $43,496.

As of 2002 the average salaries of staff nurses range from $50,000 to $65,000 per year. The higher salaries are paid on the East and West Coasts and the lower salaries in the South. Fringe benefits usually include additional compensation for evening and night shifts, paid vacation and holidays, health insurance, and often tuition reimbursement on a percentage basis and/or provisions for continuing education.

The description and function of a staff nurse in a nursing home or extended care facility are similar to that of the hospital. The extended care facility (ECF), like the nursing home, offers long-term nursing care; however, it also must provide a high level of concentrated rehabilitation services to patients. These often include the skills of occupational therapy, recreational therapy, physical therapy, and speech therapy. Staff nurses employed by an ECF usually enjoy benefits similar to those offered by hospitals; the pace, however, is usually not as hectic and intense, and the requirements for a degreed nurse are less strict.

Public Health Nurses

Public health nurses (often referred to as *community health nurses* or *visiting nurses*) may often be working in situations not unlike those of staff nurses, yet their roles and responsibilities differ greatly. Public health nurses typically spend the majority of their working time in the community, in clients' homes, in community agencies, or in schools; hence, public health nurses are more often referred to as community health nurses.

Community health nurses may be employed by a variety of agencies, including private agencies that are operated to make a profit (privately owned clinics and health care agencies); official agencies, which are operated through tax-supported and government funds (local health departments); and nonofficial agencies, which operate with funds primarily from the community (local visiting nurse organizations). Each of these agencies also employs additional health care professionals and workers.

Community or public health nurses function as links for patients between the hospital and community and as consultants, advisors, and direct care providers in community facilities. For example, public health nurses work on mobile city alcoholism treatment teams that cooperate with psychiatrists, social workers, medical residents, and alcoholism counselors.

Community or public health nurses have the opportunity to function in a wide variety of situations. However, the nature of the job requires a willingness to leave the protective environment of the hospital. In fact a number of articles in nursing journals are devoted to the topic of the safety of nurses in the community. Given the current climate in health care, most hospitals must discharge their patients earlier than ever before because of severe financial constraints. As a result the community nurse or the home health nurse often provides care and treatment to patients who are quite sick and/or require complicated treatments previously administered only in the hospital. For example, intravenous antibiotics for a bone infection are now frequently given at home. Another example is kidney dialysis or chemotherapy administered at home.

It is imperative that public health nurses can rely on their own resources and feel comfortable in clients' homes. It really is quite different from the hospital, but nurses who enjoy variety and self-reliance will find satisfaction in community health nursing. Working hours for community health nursing generally are more consistent with employment in other occupations than they are for other areas of nursing. Most agencies operate on a 9:00 A.M. to 5:00 P.M. Monday through Friday schedule, with weekends and holidays off. The average salary is about $48,000 to $52,000 annually.

Almost all nurses in public health have completed baccalaureate degrees in nursing. This is important because a B.S. program in nursing focuses directly on the knowledge and skills required for community nursing and requires at least a semester of clinical practice in the community. In some agencies, nurses without a baccalaureate degree may be hired to assist the professional nurse.

Clinical Specialists

Clinical specialists are advanced practice nurses who usually are hired by large hospitals or medical center complexes. The position of clinical specialist may be specific for one hospital setting such as pediatrics, neurology, medicine, psychiatry, or surgery, or it may focus on particular conditions found throughout the hospital on many units such as geriatrics or oncology (cancer).

Nurse clinicians or clinical specialists are considered experts in the care of patients and in the knowledge of their areas of specialization. Their role is to identify complex nursing problems and assist the staff in dealing with specific patient needs. This may be accomplished through direct patient care and/or problem-solving sessions with the staff. More often, though, specialists provide direct care that may involve working any of three shifts—days, evenings, or nights—depending on when the nursing problem occurs and the nature of the problem.

Clinical specialists must complete additional education beyond the baccalaureate level; most hold master's degrees in nursing and have some supervised clinical experience. Many of these clinical specialists complete an exam and provide evidence of their clinical knowledge and skill to become certified by the American Nurses Association or by the related specialty organization.

The average salary differs according to institution and geographical location. The average is $62,000 a year and usually includes fringe benefits such as paid vacations, holidays, sick leave benefits, and some plan of tuition reimbursement for further education.

Nursing Administration

Nursing administration entails the responsibility for coordinating and directing the activities and roles of nursing personnel and/or personnel providing nursing-related services. Included in this category are the nurse manager, the supervisor, and the director of nursing/vice president of nursing. As greater numbers of nurses earn higher degrees and demonstrate their ability to implement more sophisticated principles of administration, they will assume more positions at the administrative level. Currently some nurses are in the position of administrator in nursing homes, and a few nurses are assuming executive-level positions in universities outside of the nursing department with titles such as vice president of academic affairs.

Nurse Managers

The position of nurse manager is the first step in the progression of administrative advancement from staff nurse. However, in some institutions there may be an assistant nurse manager position that provides experience for the nurse to assume full responsibilities. The nurse manager assumes total responsibility for a designated unit for a twenty-four-hour period, including assisting and coordinating all activities for the unit that are related to nursing care. This often entails activities such as planning staff work time, ordering supplies, implementing policies and procedures, and, most important, planning and implementing patient care. It is often the nurse manager's responsibility to act as liaison between the physicians and their medical orders and the staff and the implementation of nursing care.

Approximately 75 percent of the nurse managers practicing today have at least a bachelor's degree, and there is a continuing trend toward even higher education requirements for such positions. In addition, more and more first-level nurse managers are enrolled in baccalaureate programs.

Salaries for nurse managers are very similar to those of clinical specialists, including standard fringe benefits. An annual salary of $62,158 can be accomplished at this level.

Nursing Supervisors

Nursing supervisors are responsible for coordinating and overseeing all actions related to the provision of nursing on several units and possibly the entire institution during an evening or night shift. The position of supervisor varies with the institution. Traditionally the supervisor has been more of an administrative title, but recently the position has been developing into more of a clinical and consultant role. In this role, supervisors are encouraged to assist nurse managers and their staffs with complex patient-care problems and staff personnel relationship difficulties, rather than purely policing the implementation of policy and hearing a daily report on the patients' conditions.

Nursing supervisors usually hold baccalaureate degrees in nursing, and the trend (in line with their new roles) is for them to hold master's degrees in nursing. Salaries for nursing supervisors range from $59,507 annually depending on geographic location. The fringe benefits are usually slightly better than those of nurse managers, including additional vacation time and, in some places, retirement or annuity funds.

Nursing Directors/Vice Presidents of Nursing

Nursing directors (vice presidents of nursing) are responsible for the nature and quality of all nursing care in the institution. It is their role to formulate nursing policy and procedure, direct its implementation, and evaluate the results. This becomes an almost insurmountable task, which is the reason that most directors delegate many of the decisions. However, the final outcome of any decision regarding policy or policy implementation is rightfully determined by the director. It is for this reason that many institutions also have assistant directors of major units who make recommendations and keep the directors informed on the status of their particular areas.

The role of the director of nursing is very complex, involving responsibility both to the nursing staff and to the general administrative personnel. Administrative personnel are concerned about finances, budgets, community attitudes toward the institution, public relations, and meeting criteria for certification and approval by outside agencies responsible for standards and funding. Therefore directors are concerned with budgets, with providing the best possible care within the financial structure, with meeting standards for approval, and with mediating problems with the assistant directors.

The nature of the director's position indicates that a master's or doctorate degree in nursing administration would be in order. However, the majority of administrators possess only baccalaureate degrees. Salaries for directors average $117,411 a year, with liberal fringe benefits. Most directors spend forty or more hours a week involved in direct job tasks and often an additional four to six hours with community groups, higher administrative commitments, and other professional organization activities.

Nursing Education

Nursing education continues to grow in importance. All nurses will need critical thinking skills; independent, clinical judgment; management skills; leadership skills; and, most important, organizational skills.

Nurse educators are in the very important position of providing both nursing knowledge and an understanding of educational theory. Nurse educators may teach in a variety of settings and in various capacities.

According to the American Nurses Association, there were approximately 24,059 nurses teaching in schools of nursing in 1998. There is currently a need for additional faculty to teach in nursing programs, and there are still new nursing programs opening, even though the rate has begun to stabilize. Also, the numbers of adequately prepared nurse educators in the various programs have not reached desired levels. Most schools require that nurse faculty members earn a minimum of a master's degree, and many require a doctorate. Those teaching in graduate programs must have a doctorate. These requirements are met in approximately 60 percent of the nursing programs.

Teaching nursing offers a wide variety of benefits. In most situations, faculty are hired to instruct in a particular clinical setting and teach the related nursing theory. Therefore, a nurse who has specific theoretical knowledge and clinical expertise in the area of pediatrics may elect to teach in that field of nursing. In some settings, faculty may also be hired to instruct in only one situation. For example, an instructor may teach child nursing but only in the clinical setting, whereas another instructor may teach only theory or classroom material on pediatric nursing.

According to information taken from *Nurse Educator* (1997), the overall total of estimated nursing faculty increased by 3.7 percent between 1994 and 1996. Full-time faculty increased by 2.7 percent and part-time faculty by 7.6 percent.

In 1996 the overall average (mean) number of full-time and part-time faculty was close to the average in 1994. There was a significant increase in the mean number of full-time and part-time baccalaureate and higher degree faculty. There was a significant decrease in the mean number of part-time associate degree faculty and also a significant decrease in part-time associate degree faculty. The same significance was found for full- and part-time diploma degree faculty. It was found that there were no significant changes in the number of practical/vocational nursing faculty.

Nursing faculty members are expected to assume the same responsibilities that faculty members in other departments assume within the same educational setting. It is expected that nursing faculty members will publish, conduct research, and serve on school and college committees.

The average salary for nurse educators varies depending on the type of program and the highest degree the faculty member has earned. Data collected between 1994 and 1996 found the mean annual salary for professors with a doctorate in public and private schools was $66,144 and for professors without, $59,999; for associate professors with a doctorate $64,000 and without, $60,000; for assistant professors with a doctorate $59,999 and without, $45,000. These figures have improved substantially over the last few years. The increases were the result of more assertive nursing faculty and not an indication that college faculty salaries have improved in general.

The work schedule for nurse faculty members may vary greatly depending on the type of school and the nature of the course. Teachers in diploma or practical nurse programs usually teach more hours in the hospital or clinical setting than do faculty in baccalaureate or associate degree programs. The vacation and holiday schedule is based on an academic calendar (nine to ten months), and in many baccalaureate and associate degree programs it is consistent with the college or university schedule in which the program is based. Although the specific hours for teaching are regular and usually fall within the Monday through Friday workweek, additional hours for preparation, grading papers, and other related work are not as predictable.

Teaching nursing provides a very different atmosphere from the actual practice of nursing. In most cases, the atmosphere is similar to that of an academic setting with an opportunity for exchanging ideas and advancing nursing knowledge. There is a trend developing within a number of schools of nursing that encourages and, in some cases, requires faculty to practice. To assist faculty, some schools have opened nursing clinics that provide nursing services such as health teaching groups or routine health assessments to the students on campus as well as to the local community.

Nurses, as educators, are not restricted only to institutions where formal education takes place. In-service education within hospitals, agencies, and nursing homes has assumed tremendous importance. There is a critical need for nurses to continually update their knowledge and skills because of the rapid changes and advancements that occur in the field. Also, nurses returning to work after a number of years of inactivity need additional learning if they are to provide the current level of competent nursing care. This is essentially the role of the nursing in-service educator. As educators, in-service nurses should hold a master's degree in nursing; in some institutions, however, a baccalaureate degree with additional post-degree clinical experience is acceptable. Annual salaries earned are approximately $47,160.

With the increase in the number of states requiring some form of mandatory continuing education for relicensure, there has been a rapid increase in the number of institutions, organizations, and individuals offering continuing education. Currently there are fifteen states with legislation requiring continuing education. Of these, five refer only to nurse practitioners, whereas the other ten include all registered nurses. As a result the increased competition requires that continuing education be managed more as a business rather than as an academic exercise.

Other teaching positions are available to nurses—primarily to the registered nurse—and preference in hiring usually is given to those holding baccalaureate degrees. Such positions often involve health-related public instruction.

One employer of this type of teacher is the American Cancer Society, which often hires nurses to assist in health promotion campaigns. Other such employers include the American Lung Association, American Red Cross, and certain companies whose products are related to health. The latter hire nurses to develop and market products that teach health promotion, or to educate patients, using slides or tape recorders, about the use of products in the hospital setting.

Nursing Research

Positions for nurses in the field of research are probably the least understood, the newest, and the most challenging for the future. Until the 1960s there were few nurses prepared for research jobs because most required doctorate degrees. As of 1998 there were 12,300 nurses holding doctorates—about 0.5 percent of all nurses. Considering the number of nurses with doctorates who are working in educational and administrative positions, it is not difficult to comprehend that only a few would be available for positions that focus entirely on research. However, these numbers are rapidly increasing.

Many nurse researchers are employed in hospital settings, primarily the larger medical centers. These nurses are usually involved with evaluating patient care based on new products, nursing intervention, new nursing techniques and procedures, consulting with an interdisciplinary health care research team, and designing and evaluating patient-related research.

In the academic setting there is an increase in the number of new positions in nursing research. The focus is usually on increasing and encouraging faculty to conduct research. However, with the growing numbers of nurses with doctorates, there is an increase in full-time postdoctoral research. For example, one nurse might be investigating family conflict where one member was a "night person" (most energetic after 4:00 P.M.) and another was a "day person" (least energetic after 4:00 P.M.). With the increased emphasis on advanced degrees in nursing, more nurses are engaging in research in various capacities. A cardiac intensive care nurse discovered that by educating the patient's family about the unit's procedures, the patient's level of nervousness is lowered. A cancer nurse researcher is investigating the use of hypnosis to reduce the nausea induced by toxic cancer-retardant drugs. A nurse in continuing education is examining factors that motivate nurses to use new information in their daily practice. Nurses with master's and doctorate degrees in clinical practice, research, administration, and education are designing, implementing, and evaluating research relating to many situations. This area of nursing is beginning to enjoy prominence, visibility, and significance to the entire nursing community.

Military and Volunteer Nursing

The field of nursing provides such a wide variety of opportunities that it is impossible to discuss each one in detail. With increasing sophistication, nurses are assuming new roles and positions. There is a wide range of alternatives.

Army Nurse Corps

The Army Nurse Corps is the oldest of the governmental nursing services. Nurses who join the Army Nurse Corps enter as commissioned officers if they have completed a baccalaureate degree nursing program from a school accredited by the National League for Nursing (NLN). They receive a rank of first lieutenant and, depending upon their additional education or experience, may be commissioned on entrance as captains.

Additional criteria for acceptance require nurses to be between the ages of twenty and thirty-three, registered to practice in the United States, citizens of the United States, and recommended by references for good moral and professional standing. They also must qualify according to certain physical criteria, including health status. There are certain additional exceptions, such as the acceptance of married nurses and, just recently, acceptance of those with children.

Nurses in the army may function in such capacities as providing direct clinical nursing service, teaching, in-service education, and administering or providing consultations to other governmental personnel. They may be stationed in the United States or in any other section of the world. For further information it is best to contact the local Army Nurse Corps recruiting station or the Department of the Army, U.S. Recruiting Command, Hampton, Virginia 23369.

Navy Nurse Corps

The Navy Nurse Corps accepts nurses who have graduated from state- or NLN-accredited nursing education programs of at least 108 academic weeks in duration; are registered as nurses in the

United States, the Commonwealth of Puerto Rico (a territory of the United States), or the District of Columbia; are citizens of the United States; are between the ages of twenty and thirty-four-and-a-half years; are qualified physically; and can supply references for good professional and personal standing.

Nurses in the Navy Nurse Corps may provide a variety of services, including direct care to patients, educating medical personnel in the area of patient care, instructing patients and other nurses, and administrating in positions such as head nurses. Navy Corps nurses may be assigned to the United States, to other countries, or to specific hospital or naval ships. For additional information contact the local navy recruiting station or call the navy's toll-free number, (800) 841-8000.

Air Force Nurse Corps

The Air Force Nurse Corps accepts nurses who have graduated from approved schools of nursing that award a baccalaureate degree; however, nurses graduated from programs that are at least two years in length will be considered if they have at least three years of postgraduation nursing experience. Candidates must be registered nurses who are citizens of the United States or the District of Columbia, must be between the ages of twenty and thirty-five, and must pass the regulation physical examination.

One specialty area in the Air Force Nurse Corps is the flight nurse. Flight nurses are required to pass a comprehensive one-year educational program based in Texas, which includes courses such as physiology, psychology, and care of the seriously wounded. These courses are necessary because flight nurses often are responsible for wounded and seriously ill patients during air evacuations and air transport. Flight nurses must be under thirty-seven years of age and physically certified for flying.

Another section within the Air Force Nurse Corps is aerospace nursing, a relatively new field. Like flight nurses, aerospace nurses are required to complete a one-year program that is designed to prepare nurses to function as members of medical teams for space flights. In addition, they are taught to implement and evaluate research on the effects of stress on the human organism. This research is carried out under the auspices of the Bioastronautic Operational Support Unit. The local air force recruiter will have additional information and be able to supply further details necessary for applying to the Air Force Nurse Corps.

All of the nursing programs of the armed services have a plan that provides some financial assistance for the basic nursing preparation. Such information may be obtained from the recruiting station or from the department of that specific branch that is in charge of nurse recruitment.

Peace Corps Nurses

Peace Corps nurses also are given opportunities for travel and adventure. The Peace Corps, initiated in 1961 by President Kennedy, accepts registered nurses who are citizens of the United States or the District of Columbia. They must have completed at least three years of experience as nurses in a clinical setting, have a driver's license, and pass a very rigorous and stringent physical and psychological examination. Peace Corps nurses represent the United States in the name of promoting peace between the United States and any one of approximately sixty countries and, therefore, are screened very carefully.

Prior to assignment, Peace Corps nurses undergo training for overseas service, including language instruction appropriate for the country of assignment.

On the job, Peace Corps nurses may be responsible for nursing other Peace Corps volunteers, planning and implementing health care, teaching in towns and villages, instructing health care workers in local clinics or hospitals, or providing administrative assistance to a health-related facility. Tours of duty last two years, followed by a rest in the United States. If desired, another two-year assignment to another country may be arranged.

Peace Corps nurses enjoy excellent benefits, including liberal vacations with arrangements for travel and provision of housing where assigned. Certainly the people-to-people aspect of Peace Corps service and the satisfaction of providing much-needed nursing care are important factors for applicants to consider.

VISTA is the domestic equivalent of the Peace Corps. Nurses who are accepted as volunteers work in areas plagued by general poverty and poor health. These areas may be in the United States, Puerto Rico, or the Virgin Islands. VISTA nurses typically have been assigned to work in settings such as migrant worker farms, Indian reservations, Appalachia, or poverty pockets in large cities. Nurses in VISTA sign up for a year and many continue for a second year in the same locale. Write to Peace Corps/VISTA, Washington, D.C. 20525 for further information about both programs.

Project HOPE also offers interesting work to nurses who have graduated from accredited nursing programs, are licensed to practice, and can meet character criteria. HOPE programs, based until 1974 on the hospital ship SS *Hope*, now consist chiefly of land-based medical teaching and training programs. For information write to Project HOPE, 2233 Wisconsin Avenue NW, Washington, D.C. 20007.

Nursing Practice Specialties

There are several other practitioners of nursing who do not fit into the usual categories and can be distinguished either by where they practice or by what type of nurse they are. These include nurse practitioners, nurse-midwives, psychiatric-mental health practitioners, geriatric nurse practitioners, family nurse practitioners, private duty nurses, occupational nurses, industrial nurses, school nurses, nurse anesthetists, office nurses, case management nurses, diabetes nurses, emergency room nurses, infection control nurses, pediatric nurse practitioners, rehabilitation nurses, and orthopedic nurses. Some descriptions follow.

Nurse Practitioners

With the age of specialization in health care and the tremendous need for the delivery of improved, competent health services, nurses have assumed positions that utilize the full extent of their skills and knowledge. A number of specific health care areas employ nurse practitioners, whose responsibilities include detailed taking and assembling of health history, teaching, and providing related therapies in collaboration with physicians, physical therapists, and other members of the health care team. There are currently a number of demonstration projects in which the nurse practitioner is the primary health care provider giving care and treatment in the clinic as well as in the hospital. Almost all states have approved provisions for nurse practitioners to write prescriptions. As of 1998 there were 51,500 nurse practitioners and more than 150 master's programs offering nurse practitioner specialization.

In *Dimensions of Professional Nursing*, Lucie Kelly points out that for the most part, "it is conceded that nurse practitioners have acquired additional medical knowledge and skills, whether in short-term or degree educational programs, and use fully all aspects of nursing skills, which enable them to provide more extensive health services to the patient/client, often in collaboration with a physician as needed." It is on this basis that some nurses contend that the nurse practitioner is actually functioning as a physician's assistant—utilizing more medical knowledge and skills than in nursing. However, even though the techniques and information are similar to those used by the physician, the nurse practitioner is expected to use the information in a different manner. For example, there is a much greater emphasis on health teaching and physical assessment as a part of a home visit. In some remote or underserved areas, the nurse practitioner may be the only source of daily health care.

The place and nature of employment of nurse practitioners vary greatly. Some are employed in hospital settings and may be responsible for initial health screening in a clinic. Others, such as pediatric nurse practitioners, focus on children, performing physical assessments and teaching normal child development to parents.

There are a number of different types of nurse practitioners, and this number is increasing. At present, the most common types are adult nurse practitioners, pediatric nurse practitioners, family nurse practitioners, and geriatric nurse practitioners. Also available are additional specialties such as acute care, neonatology, oncology, emergency room, and home care. For each there is an educational program available that offers preparation for the position. However, there is often variation in the length of study (from six months to two years) and in the theory and experience content. Programs may be hospital-, medical-, or nursing-school based, and some offer a certificate of completion while others award a master's degree. Since there is so much variation, it is important to gather as much information as possible regarding the particular area of interest. The American Nurses Association and National League for Nursing, in addition to specific school and program bulletins, will provide the best information.

For certification in the specialty area (required by most states in order to write prescriptions) in almost all instances, a master's degree is required. The average salary in 2000 was $63,600, although salary is rapidly rising as the need for such nurses to provide health care rises.

Nurse-Midwives

Nurse-midwives, along with community health nurses, were probably the first nurse practitioners in the true sense of the definition. Nurse-midwives assess and care for mothers and their families throughout the total pregnancy period and follow up in normal and uncomplicated cases. Nurse-midwives contact expectant mothers during the earliest stages of pregnancy and monitor them throughout the ensuing months to be sure that the pregnancy is progressing normally. Additionally, nurse-midwives provide instruction to the mother, father, and other family members in areas such as family adjustment, diet, exercise, proper clothing, and emotional adjustment. During labor and delivery, nurse-midwives provide assistance and support to the women and watch for signs that a physician's attention is required. They care for and observe babies when they are born and instruct parents about how to take care of infants.

It is important to note that nurse-midwives deal only with normal and uncomplicated pregnancies. (Ninety-six percent of the births and deliveries in the United States are normal.) Additionally, nurse-midwives work in association with obstetricians and, therefore, are considered somewhat dependent on the physician for their practice. In 1990 they delivered 148,728 babies—about 3.6 percent of all births in the United States that year.

Nurse-midwives are licensed registered nurses who have completed additional education and have had experience in a nurse-midwifery program approved by the American College of Nurse-Midwives (ACNM). They must pass an examination to become certified nurse-midwives. Such midwifery programs may be hospital-based or in a medical or nursing school and may award a certificate of completion or a master's degree. However, education for certification increasingly is requiring that it be at the master's level.

It is important to consider the requirements for entry into each program early because they do vary. Some require certain courses for admission, and others want applicants to have had certain clinical experiences. It is important to be aware of a program's prerequisites, because there are more nurses interested in this specialty area than the programs have room to accommodate. The average salary in 2000 was $63,200.

For further information write to:

American College of Nurse-Midwives
1012 Fourteenth Street NW, Suite 801
Washington, D.C. 20005

Psychiatric-Mental Health Practitioners

Psychiatric-mental health practitioners of nursing provide nursing intervention for clients' emotional needs in settings such as community mental health centers, crisis intervention clinics, and psychiatric institutions. Education determines at what level and in what situations these nurses may function.

Usually nurses with associate degrees function in well-supervised psychiatric settings. Nurses with baccalaureate degrees in nursing are prepared to function more independently and assist with crisis intervention and ongoing mental health counseling in mental health centers or psychiatric institutions. Nurses with master's degrees in psychiatric or mental health nursing are considered clinical specialists and are prepared to carry private caseloads in settings such as community mental health centers or community health agencies. This area of nursing enables nurses to provide nursing intervention in a very independent manner.

Some psychiatric or mental health nurses, upon completion of their specialized master's program, decide to pursue the area of psychiatric mental health nursing as private practitioners. They often accomplish this by attending programs that provide additional theory and clinical experience in areas such as group, individual, or family therapy.

Geriatric Nurse Practitioners

The geriatric nurse practitioner enters a field that in general has great promise and potential for the future. The age group over sixty-five has been rising rapidly for several decades and currently stands at about thirty million. A study by the Rand Corporation accurately predicted that by 1990 there would be a tremendous shortage of professionals to meet the health care needs of the elderly. This certainly is still the case today.

The geriatric nurse practitioner functions primarily in community settings, although there is a trend toward the use of geriatric nurse practitioners in nursing homes and as a part of the patient care team for the hospitalized elderly. Their responsibilities include securing and evaluating history, physical findings, and laboratory data related to the older patient's status; providing information and support to older patients and their families; enlisting appropriate referral resources to aid the older patient and family with health promotion or coping with illness; and providing social, physical, and/or emotional rehabilitation to the chronically ill patient and/or family.

Family Nurse Practitioners

Family nurse practitioners function as the primary providers of health care in a wide variety of settings such as rural and remote clinics, neighborhood health centers, joint practice with physicians, outpatient departments, and as private practitioners. Educational programs preparing family nurse practitioners place great importance on family dynamics and family therapy skills. Responsibilities include activities such as assessing and managing well and minimally ill children; managing uncomplicated pregnancies prior to and following birth; providing teaching and examinations for family planning; supervising the medical care of patients whose illness has stabilized and recognizing signs of complications that require the physician; and providing acute and emergency care depending on the situation.

The extent of responsibility that is assumed by the family nurse practitioner is somewhat dependent on the setting. A nurse in a rural and remote area of New Mexico or Utah may have only telephone contact with a physician, in conjunction with weekly visits. In a large urban setting, the physician and nurse may be in joint practice with access to each other on a face-to-face, daily basis.

Private Duty Nurses

Private duty nurses are self-employed and function as private practitioners. They are actually hired by the patient or family for whom they will provide nursing services. These services may be in the hospital setting or in a home. Private duty nurses usually attend to only one or two patients and are responsible for their total care. Most of these patients are in a hospital setting and usually require complex care because they are returning from complicated surgery, are highly emotional, or are critically ill.

Private duty nurses usually register with an appropriate registry or the local hospital and are assigned cases from these sources. Some nurses also rely on physicians, nurses, or other personal contacts for patient referrals. They usually charge on a daily or hourly basis, and their fees are regulated to some degree by the local hospital (but primarily by the professional registries). However, private duty nurses legally are permitted to charge according to personal discretion. As in any case of self-employment, there are no fringe benefits, and vacation scheduling and insurance coverage are the responsibility of the individual.

Occupational and Industrial Nurses

Occupational health nurses and industrial nurses are also to some extent independent practitioners; however, often they ultimately are responsible to a physician who is employed as medical director or consultant by the employing firm.

Occupational health nurses work in places such as department stores, large companies, and factories. Their primary responsibility is to promote health, prevent disease, and assist with the rehabilitation of sick or injured employees in the firm. Occupational health nurses are concerned mainly with the general work environment, and through teaching, counseling, and modification of the environment, they focus on health promotion.

As independent nurse practitioners, it is essential for occupational health nurses to have baccalaureate degrees in nursing. However, this is not required and most do not have a degree. Occupational health nurses earn on the average $42,722 yearly and usually receive fringe benefits such as insurance and retirement plans and the same vacation and holiday time as managerial employees.

School Nurses

Nurses who provide services within a school system function in a variety of situations. The main responsibility of school nurses is to promote the health and well-being of the students and prevent illness. School nurses are hired by the community board of education and, therefore, are subject to the same rules, regulations, and benefits as are the other employees and teachers. School nurses attend faculty meetings and participate in school activities in collaboration with the other professional employees. Many nurses whose own children reach school age find this job particularly appealing, because their hours and vacation time usually coincide with those of their children.

School nurses act as health consultants to other faculty and to parents and students. They are responsible for advising faculty about signs and symptoms that might indicate a deviation from health as well as for providing instruction regarding an emotionally and physically healthy environment at home and school. School nurses also alert parents about potential or actual student health problems. For example, the school nurse may notify parents about their child's below-normal scores on a hearing test.

School nurses also are responsible for implementing sections of the state health code that relate to students in a school setting. This usually requires nurses to record and monitor immunizations and to participate in the prevention of communicable diseases. As school representatives it is also important for school nurses to work with the community's hospitals, clinics, and other health personnel.

A bachelor's degree in nursing is considered minimum preparation for school nursing. In addition to being licensed as registered professional nurses, school nurses must also meet any additional state or local school requirements. The salaries of school nurses are in line with those of other teachers and faculty who have similar educational preparation and experience. The average salary is currently in the vicinity of $34,763 for a nine- to ten-month academic year.

For further information about school nursing write to either of the following organizations:

American School Health Association
ASHA Building
Kent, Ohio 44240

Department of School Nurses
National Education Association
1201 Sixteenth Street NW
Washington, D.C. 20036

In addition, many areas have a local school nurses' group that is usually quite pleased to supply information. School nurses in the local school system also would be able to provide assistance.

Nurse Anesthetists

Licensed registered nurses who are interested in administering anesthesia, preparing patients for surgery or major procedures, and following up the effects of the anesthesia would probably be interested in becoming nurse anesthetists. The course of study is approximately two years in length and includes lectures on the theory of anesthesia and its administration in conjunction with supervised experience of actually administering the anesthesia to patients. As of 1996, programs in nurse anesthesia must be part of educational units that offer a master's degree. Schools that offer such courses are based in approximately two hundred hospitals across the country. Most charge tuition but also provide small incomes for the services students provide by administering anesthesia to hospital patients. A list of such schools and further information may be obtained from:

American Association of Nurse Anesthetists
222 South Prospect Avenue
Park Ridge, Illinois 60068-4001

Following completion of the program of anesthesia, nurses must then pass a certifying examination that tests their knowledge of anesthesia and the functions of a nurse anesthetist.

Nurse anesthetists are hired to work in hospitals, operating and emergency rooms, surgical clinics, and dentists' offices. Sixty-five percent of all anesthetics are administered by certified registered nurse anesthetists; they are the only providers in 85 percent of rural hospitals. There is usually a greater demand for their services in smaller hospitals and in rural settings. Nurse anesthetists usually work in conjunction with physicians or dentists, who may or may not actually be present.

Anesthetists' salaries are higher than average nursing salaries. In 2000 the average salary was $97,500. However, nurse anesthetists often are on call and may be assigned to work irregular shifts and holidays.

Private Practice

As nurses continue to improve their level of sophistication and educational background, the idea of private practice becomes more attractive and plausible. A nurse in private practice provides nursing services as an independent agent outside of an institution or agency. The individual or individuals, in the case of a group practice, identify the scope of the practice, determine and collect fees directly, assume total responsibilities for the care provided, and establish their own referral system.

The type of private practice is determined by the expertise of the nurse. One group of nurses offered kidney dialysis services in a mobile unit to small hospitals that ordinarily could not afford them independently, whereas another group provided a range of health promoting services, including weight and stress reduction groups. In another situation, a nurse joined an interdisciplinary group of psychologists, social workers, and marriage counselors, and another joined a group of neurosurgeons to provide teaching and support to the families of neurosurgical patients.

One problem that reduces the attractiveness of private practice is the current lack of coverage by insurance companies of private, independent nurses or services. Most health professionals do not provide the range of services that nurses do, such as home visits, and clients are often willing to pay for them without insurance coverage. A number of states, through the state nurses association or special interest groups, have influenced the passage of legislation to cover these nursing services through insurance.

6

NURSING ORGANIZATIONS

AFTER NURSES HAVE graduated and are licensed to practice, they should become members of nursing organizations or nursing-related organizations associated with their specialties. Only through such membership and active participation can professional goals be realized. Early in their careers, nurses might ask, "Why should I join? What will a national organization do for me?"

To answer these questions, it is necessary to understand what an organization is and what its functions are. An organization is simply a group of people united together to achieve a common purpose. The tasks undertaken by such groups are beyond the capabilities of individuals acting alone; however, by pooling individual talents and resources, a group can act to accomplish its organizational goals.

There are generally two kinds of organizational structures—the professional and the nonprofessional. According to one definition by R. K. Merton in the *American Journal of Nursing*, "A professional organization is an organization of practitioners who judge one another as professionally competent and who have banded together to perform social functions which they cannot perform in their separate capacities as individuals." An example of this is the American Nurses Association (ANA). This is the major professional organization for registered nurses because only nurses may join. The nonprofessional nursing organization is the National League for Nursing (NLN). Its membership is made up of all kinds of people—nurses at all levels as well as non-nurses. The specific interest of this group is health, with a focus on nursing. These are the two largest national organizations concerned with nurses and nursing, and they have been planned so that their functions and activities mesh but do not overlap.

Over the years there have evolved many other organizations related to nursing and health. Some are totally independent specialty organizations for nurses; others are part of a medical or educational organization. Some restrict membership to nurses; others include medical-technical personnel employed in the same clinical specialty. Examples of these organizations are: the American Association of Critical Care Nurses, the American Association of Industrial Nurses, the American Association of Nephrology Nurses and Technicians, the American Association of Nurse Anesthetists, the American Association of Neurosurgical Nurses, the American College of Nurse-Midwives, the American Urological Association, the Association of Operating Room Nurses, the Department of School Nurses of the National Education Association, the American Association of Colleges of Nursing, the National Black Nurses Association, and the Nurses' Christian Fellowship. It is entirely possible that still more nursing organizations will be developed over the years as the role of the nurse continues to evolve and expand to meet the health care needs of the consumer in an ever-changing society.

When joining any organization, it is helpful to know how the organization meets its objectives. The following descriptions of some important nursing organizations explain their functions and how they achieve their objectives.

American Nurses Association

The American Nurses Association is the national professional organization for registered nurses in the United States. It is one of the largest professional organizations in the country and is composed of nurses associations of the fifty states, the District of Columbia, the Virgin Islands, and Guam. The national association takes care of those matters related to all nurses throughout the United States; the state-level associations activate nurses in a given state to recognize and meet the needs of their nurses at that level. State organizations are broken down into districts, which are usually determined geographically according to specific areas; this usually is the point at which membership starts. The district office provides information about district, state, and national dues. At all levels there remains the ultimate purpose, or function, of the ANA—to promote the welfare and the professional and educational advancement of nurses to the end that all people may have better nursing care.

Membership, which is limited to registered nurses, enables nurses to become acquainted with colleagues and to share points of view on nursing on a national and international basis. Nurses' own professional growth and development are enhanced through contributions made toward the general welfare of all nurses; the advancement of nursing practice, nursing service, and nursing education; and the formulation of policies in connection with national nursing affairs. As a result of the ANA's efforts over the years, nurses now receive Social Security benefits, work eight-hour days, and receive salaries and other benefits comparable with other professional fields.

National League for Nursing

The National League for Nursing is an organization of professional and nonprofessional individuals and agencies. The purpose of the NLN is "to foster the development and improvement of hospital, industrial, public health, and other organized nursing service and of nursing education through the coordinated action of nurses, allied professional groups, citizens, agencies, and schools, to the end that the nursing needs of the people will be met." Members of this group may be registered or practical nurses, nurses' aides, allied health workers, interested lay- and businesspeople, government workers, and patients. This broad membership increases the NLN's available resources and effectiveness in solving problems confronting nursing service and nursing education.

The goals of the NLN are achieved through its services of defining the nursing needs of society; fostering programs designed to meet these needs; and providing research studies, evaluations, consultations, interpretations, testing services, publications, and accreditation. All of these foster cooperation between nursing education and nursing service as well as between consumer expectations and nursing service.

The NLN provides accreditation services for both professional and practical schools of nursing. Through this mechanism, the NLN strives to attain and maintain quality preparation for practice. It is desirable for a school to earn national accreditation because this will project an image of high standards for the institution.

International Council of Nurses

When a nurse joins the ANA, membership in another organization called the International Council of Nurses (ICN) becomes automatic, as a small percentage of ANA dues is paid to this federation of national nursing organizations. The purpose of ICN is to provide a means for national nurses associations to share common interests while working together to develop and contribute to the promotion of health and care of the ill throughout the world. ICN represents and facilitates the work of nurses and nursing on the international level. It is nursing's ambassador abroad.

Sigma Theta Tau

The national honor society in nursing, comparable to the national honor societies in other professions, is Sigma Theta Tau. This organization has as its purpose the recognition of superior achievement and the development of leadership, fostering of high professional standards, encouragement of creativity, and strengthening of commitment to professional ideals and purposes.

Invitation to membership is offered to graduate nurses of a baccalaureate or higher-degree program. Selection may also be made on the basis of outstanding achievements or contributions made to the profession.

The society maintains a research fund through which grants can be awarded to nurses engaged in doctoral research. Many local chapters offer scholarships to students in nursing. This organization provides the basis for major contributions to the field.

Academy of Nursing

The Academy of Nursing is the organization that recognizes professional achievement and excellence. Its purpose is "the advancement of knowledge, education, and nursing practice." Since the fellows of the academy are the leaders in the profession, this is an innovative and influential group in nursing.

The overlying function in all of these organizations is to guarantee the quality of professional growth and development while assuring the consumer of equivalent health care service. When the need is recognized, it is the professional organization's responsibility to work for legislative changes that will assist the practitioner, educator, and the public to acquire acceptable standards of health care.

There are well over two million nurses in the United States. With these astounding numbers, the nursing profession wields a great deal of potential power. Involvement of large, active membership in nursing organizations at local, state, and national levels will produce the impact necessary to convince legislators of nursing's professional purpose.

Nurses today are becoming increasingly aware, active, and politically conscious; thus, they project more than ever before an image of professional self-respect—the kind of public image nursing needs. As the profession continues its evolution in this direction, its full potential will be realized, and the American public will receive the health care to which it is entitled at an affordable price. This is the ultimate goal in organizing nurses to function in their capacity as nurses and as citizens.

Appendix A

State Nurses Associations

(NOTE: IT IS best to check the address of the state board of nursing that you are interested in since addresses may change; also try the Internet for more information.)

American Nurses Association
600 Maryland Ave. SW, Ste.
100W
Washington, DC 20024

Alabama State Nurses
Association
360 N. Hull St.
Montgomery, AL 36104

Alaska Nurses Association
2207 E. Tudor Rd., Ste. 34
Anchorage, AK 99501

Arizona Nurses Association
1850 E. Southern Ave., Ste. 1
Tempe, AZ 85282

Arkansas Nurses Association
117 S. Cedar St.
Little Rock, AR 72205

California Nurses Association
1145 Market St., Ste. 1100
San Francisco, CA 94103

Colorado Nurses Association
5453 E. Evans Pl.
Denver, CO 80222

Connecticut Nurses Association
Meritech Business Park
377 Research Pkwy., Ste. 2D
Meriden, CT 06450

Delaware Nurses Association
2634 Capitol Trail, Ste. A
Newark, DE 19711

District of Columbia Nurses
    Association
5100 Wisconsin Ave. NW, Ste.
    306
Washington, DC 20016

Florida Nurses Association
P.O. Box 536985
Orlando, FL 32853

Georgia Nurses Association
3032 Briarcliff Rd. NE
Atlanta, GA 30309

Guam Nurses Association
P.O. Box 3134
Agana, GU 96910

Hawaii Nurses Association
677 Ala Moana Blvd., Ste. 301
Honolulu, HI 96813

Idaho Nurses Association
200 N. Fourth St., Ste. 20
Boise, ID 83702

Illinois Nurses Association
105 W. Adams St., Ste. 2101
Chicago, IL 60603

Indiana State Nurses Association
2915 N. High School Rd.
Indianapolis, IN 46224

Iowa Nurses Association
1501 Forty-Second St., Ste. 471
West Des Moines, IA 50266

Kansas State Nurses Association
1208 SW Tyler
Topeka, KS 66612

Kentucky Nurses Association
1400 S. First St.
P.O. Box 2616
Louisville, KY 40201

Louisiana State Nurses
    Association
5700 Florida Blvd., Ste. 720
Baton Rouge, LA 70806

ANA-Maine
P.O. Box 254
Auburn, ME 04212

Maryland Nurses Association
849 International Dr.
Airport Square 21, Ste. 255
Linthicum, MD 21090

Massachusetts Association of
    Registered Nurses
345 Greenwood St.
Worcester, MA 01607

Michigan Nurses Association
2310 Jolly Oak Rd.
Okemos, MI 48864

Minnesota Nurses Association
1625 Energy Park Dr.
St. Paul, MN 55108

Mississippi Nurses Association
31 Woodgreen Pl.
Madison, MS 39110

Missouri Nurses Association
1904 Bubba Lane
Jefferson City, MO 65110

Montana Nurses Association
104 Broadway, Ste. G-2
Helena, MT 59601

Nebraska Nurses Association
715 S. Fourteenth St.
Lincoln, NE 68508

Nevada Nurses Association
P.O. Box 34660
Reno, NV 89533

New Hampshire Nurses
   Association
48 West St.
Concord, NH 03301

New Jersey State Nurses
   Association
1479 Pennington Rd.
Trenton, NJ 08618

New Mexico Nurses Association
P.O. Box 29658
Santa Fe, NM 87592

New York State Nurses
   Association
11 Cornell Rd.
Latham, NY 12110

North Carolina Nurses
   Association
103 Enterprise St.
Raleigh, NC 27605

North Dakota Nurses
   Association
531 Airport Rd., Ste. D
Bismarck, ND 58504

Ohio Nurses Association
4000 E. Main St.
Columbus, OH 43213

Oklahoma Nurses Association
6414 N. Santa Fe, Ste. A
Oklahoma City, OK 73116

Oregon Nurses Association
9600 SW Oak, Ste. 550
Portland, OR 97223

Pennsylvania Nurses Association
2578 Interstate Dr.
Harrisburg, PA 17110

Rhode Island State Nurses
   Association
300 Ray Dr., Ste. 5
Providence, RI 02906

South Carolina Nurses
   Association
1821 Gadsden St.
Columbia, SC 29201

South Dakota Nurses Association
1505 S. Minnesota Ave., Ste. 3
Sioux Falls, SD 57105

Tennessee Nurses Association
545 Mainstream Dr., Ste. 405
Nashville, TN 37228

Texas Nurses Association
7600 Burnet Rd., Ste. 440
Austin, TX 78757

Utah Nurses Association
455 E. 400 S, Ste. 402
Salt Lake City, UT 84111

Vermont State Nurses Association
Box 26
Champlain Mill, 1 Main St.
Winooski, VT 05404

Virgin Islands State Nurses
   Association
P.O. Box 583
Christiansted, St. Croix
U.S. Virgin Islands 00821

Virginia Nurses Association
7113 Three Chopt Rd., Ste. 204
Richmond, VA 23226

Washington State Nurses
   Association
2505 Second Ave., Ste. 500
Seattle, WA 98121

West Virginia Nurses Association
P.O. Box 1946
Charleston, WV 25327

Wisconsin Nurses Association
6117 Monona Dr.
Madison, WI 53716

Wyoming Nurses Association
Majestic Building, Rm. 305
1603 Capital Ave.
Cheyenne, WY 82001

APPENDIX B

State Boards of Nursing

(NOTE: IT IS best to check the address of the state board of nursing that you are interested in since addresses may change; also try the Internet for more information.)

Alabama Board of Nursing
One/East Building, Ste. 203
500 E. Blvd.
Montgomery, AL 36117

Alaska Board of Nursing
Dept. of Commerce and Economic Development
Div. of Occupational Licensing
P.O. Box D-LIC
Juneau, AK 99811-0800

Arizona State Board of Nursing
2001 W. Camelback Rd., Ste. 350
Phoenix, AZ 85015

Arkansas Board of Nursing
1123 S. University Ave., Ste. 800
Little Rock, AR 72204

California Board of Registered Nursing
1030 Thirteenth St., Ste. 200
Sacramento, CA 94244-2100

Colorado Board of Nursing
1560 Broadway, Ste. 670
Denver, CO 80202

Connecticut Department of Health Services, Nurse Licensure
150 Washington St.
Hartford, CT 06106

Delaware Board of Nursing
P.O. Box 1401
Dover, DE 19901

Florida Board of Nursing
111 E. Coastline Dr., Ste. 504
Jacksonville, FL 32202

Georgia Board of Nursing
166 Pryor St. SW, Ste. 400
Atlanta, GA 30303

Hawaii Board of Nursing
P.O. Box 3469
Honolulu, HI 96801

Idaho Board of Nursing
500 S. Tenth St., Ste. 102
Boise, ID 83720

Illinois Nursing Committee
Dept. of Registration and Educa-
    tion
320 W. Washington St.
Springfield, IL 62786

Indiana State Board of Nursing
One American Square, Ste. 1020
Indianapolis, IN 46282-0001

Iowa Board of Nursing
State Office Bldg.
1223 E. Court
Des Moines, IA 50319

Kansas Board of Nursing
900 SW Jackson, Ste. 551-S
Topeka, KS 66612-1256

Kentucky Board of Nursing
4010 Dupont Circle, Ste. 430
Louisville, KY 40207

Louisiana State Board of Nursing
150 Baronne St., Rm. 907
New Orleans, LA 70112

Maine Board of Nursing
295 Water St.
Augusta, ME 04330-2240

Maryland Board of Examiners of
    Nurses
4201 Patterson Ave.
Baltimore, MD 21215-2299

Massachusetts Board of
    Registration in Nursing
100 Cambridge St., Rm. 1519
Boston, MA 02202

Michigan Board of Nursing
611 N. Otiana
Lansing, MI 48909

Minnesota Board of Nursing
2700 University Ave. W, Ste. 108
St. Paul, MN 55114

Mississippi Board of Nursing
239 Lamar St., Ste. 401
Jackson, MS 39201

Missouri Board of Nursing
3524 N. Ten Mile Dr.
Jefferson City, MO 65102

Montana Board of Nurses
Dept. of Commerce
1424 Ninth Ave.
Helena, MT 59620-0407

Nebraska Board of Nursing
Dept. of Health, Bureau of
   Examining Boards
P.O. Box 95007
Lincoln, NE 68509

Nevada Board of Nursing
1281 Terminal Way, Ste. 116
Reno, NV 89502

New Hampshire Board of
   Nursing
Education and Registration
6 Hazen Dr.
Concord, NH 03301

New Jersey Board of Nursing
1101 Raymond Blvd., Rm. 508
Newark, NJ 07102

New Mexico Board of Nursing
4253 Montgomery NE, Ste. 130
Albuquerque, NM 87109

New York Board of Nursing
State Education Dept.
Cultural Education Center
Albany, NY 12230

North Carolina Board of
   Nursing
P.O. Box 2129
Raleigh, NC 27602

North Dakota Board of Nursing
Kirkwood Office Tower
7th and Arbor Ave., Ste. 504
Bismarck, ND 58504

Ohio Board of Nursing
   Education and Registration
77 S. High St.
Columbus, OH 43266-0316

Oklahoma Board of Nurse
   Registration and Nursing
   Education
2915 N. Classen Blvd., Ste. 524
Oklahoma City, OK 73106

Oregon Board of Nursing
1400 SW Fifth Ave., Ste. 904
Portland, OR 97201

Pennsylvania Board of Nurse
   Examiners
P.O. Box 2649
Harrisburg, PA 17105-2649

Rhode Island Board of Nurse
   Education and Registration
Cannon Health Bldg.
75 Davis St., Ste. 104
Providence, RI 02908

South Carolina Board of Nursing
1777 St. Julian Pl., Ste. 102
Columbia, SC 29204

South Dakota Board of Nursing
304 S. Phillips Ave., Ste. 205
Sioux Falls, SD 57102

Tennessee Board of Nursing
283 Plus Park Blvd.
Nashville, TN 37219-5407

Texas Board of Nurse Examiners
9101 Burnet Rd., Ste. 104
Austin, TX 78758

Utah Board of Nursing
160 E., 300 S.
Salt Lake City, UT 84145

Vermont Board of Nursing
26 Terrace St.
Montpelier, VT 05602

Virginia Board of Nursing
1601 Rolling Hills Dr.
Richmond, VA 23229

Washington Board of Nursing
Division of Professional Licensing
P.O. Box 9649
Olympia, WA 98504

Washington, D.C. Nurses'
Examining Board
614 H St. NW, Rm. 904
Washington, DC 20001

West Virginia Board of
Examiners
922 Quarrier St., Ste. 309
Charleston, WV 25301

Wisconsin Board of Nursing
P.O. Box 8935, Rm. 174
Madison, WI 53708

Wyoming Board of Nursing
Barret Bldg., 3rd Floor
2301 Central Ave.
Cheyenne, WY 82002

BIBLIOGRAPHY

Master's Education in Nursing: Route to Opportunities in Contemporary Nursing. Publication No. 15-1312. New York: National League for Nursing Press, 1997.

McCloskey, J., and H. Grace. *Current Issues in Nursing.* St. Louis, Mo.: Mosby, 1997.

Nurse Careers in the Veteran's Administration. Washington, D.C.: Veteran's Administration, 1999.

Nurse Educators: 1997. New York: National League for Nursing, 1999.

Nursing Data Review: 1994. Publication No. 19-2639. New York: Division of Research, National League for Nursing Press, 1996.

Nursing Data Review: 1997. New York: National League for Nursing, 1999.

Nursing Data Source: 1997. Vol. 1. *Trends in Contemporary R.N. Nursing Education.* New York: National League for Nursing, 1999.

Official Guide to Undergraduate and Graduate Nursing Schools.
New York: National League for Nursing and Jones &
Bartlett Publishers (Sudberg, Mass.), 2000.

Scholarships and Loans for Beginning Education in Nursing. New
York: National League for Nursing Press, 1999.

Source Book, The Registered Nurse Population. Washington, D.C.:
U.S. Department of Health, Education, and Welfare Public
Health Service, 1994.

Standards for Nursing Practice. Washington, D.C.: American
Nurses Association (available for different nursing specialties
such as medical-surgical nursing, gerontology, and so forth).

U.S. Department of Health and Human Services, Centers for
Disease Control and Prevention. *Active Nursing Personnel
Practicing in the United States in the Last Twenty Years.* Wash-
ington, D.C.: National Center for Health Statistics, 2001.

appointed professor of nursing, associate dean for faculty and academic affairs at Pace University, Pleasantville, New York, Lienhard School of Nursing. She is professor and formerly the director of the graduate program, Lehman College of the City University of New York, and visiting professor, Teachers College of Columbia University.

Additionally, Dr. Frederickson is a consultant on nursing textbooks and serves on various nursing educational and research committees locally, nationally, and internationally. Her publications include articles and reviews that have appeared in journals such as the *Nursing Science Quarterly*, the *American Journal of Nursing*, and *Nursing Outlook*. She has also written an instructor's manual that accompanies a fundamentals-of-nursing text. Dr. Frederickson also maintained a private practice as a nurse-psychotherapist and has given numerous workshops and written chapters for books on private nursing practice, psychiatric/mental health nursing, and nursing practice models. She is a member of the National Academy of Practice in Nursing and a fellow in the American Academy of Nursing.

About the Author

Keville Frederickson completed her baccalaureate degree in nursing at Columbia University's School of Nursing and was subsequently employed at Columbia-Presbyterian Medical Center as a staff nurse and then as a head nurse.

From 1967 to 1970 she taught nursing at Columbia University in various clinical areas such as neurology, ophthalmology, medicine, and surgery.

In 1970 she completed her master's of education in psychiatric/mental health nursing at the Teachers College of Columbia University and assumed the position of in-service instructor at Columbia-Presbyterian Medical Center in the ophthalmologic unit. In 1971 she returned to the School of Nursing at Columbia to teach psychiatric/mental health nursing as an assistant professor.

In 1974, after receiving her doctoral degree in nursing education at the Teachers College of Columbia University, Dr. Frederickson joined the faculty in the division of nursing at the New York University, where she was an associate professor and director of the Center for Continuing Education in Nursing. She was then